IT'S ABOUT TIME

America's Imprisonment Binge

CONTEMPORARY ISSUES IN CRIME AND JUSTICE SERIES

Roy Roberg, San Jose State University
Series Editor

Hard Time: Understanding and Reforming the Prison (1987)
Robert Johnson, The American University

The Myth of a Racist Criminal Justice System (1987)
William Wilbanks, Florida International University

Gambling Without Guilt: The Legitimation of an American Pastime (1988)
John Rosecrance, University of Nevada at Reno

Crime Victims: An Introduction to Victimology, Second Edition (1990)
Andrew Karmen, John Jay College of Criminal Justice

Death Work: A Study of the Modern Execution Process (1990)
Robert Johnson, The American University

Lawlessness and Reform: The FBI in Transition (1990)
Tony G. Poveda, State University of New York at Plattsburgh

Women, Prison, and Crime (1990)
Joycelyn M. Pollock-Byrne, University of Houston–Downtown

Perspectives on Terrorism (1991)
Harold J. Vetter, Portland State University
Gary R. Perlstein, Portland State University

Serial Murders and Their Victims (1991)
Eric W. Hickey, California State University, Fresno

Girls, Delinquency, and the Juvenile Justice System (1992)
Meda Chesney-Lind, University of Hawaii, Manoa
Randall G. Sheldon, University of Nevada at Las Vegas

Juries and Politics (1992)
James P. Levine, Brooklyn College

Media, Crime, and Criminal Justice: Images and Realities (1992)
Ray Surette, Florida International University

Street Kids, Street Drugs, Street Crime: An Examination of Drug Use and Serious Delinquency in Miami (1993)
James A. Inciardi, University of Delaware
Ruth Horowitz, University of Delaware
Anne E. Pottieger, University of Delaware

Ethics in Crime and Justice: Dilemmas and Decisions, Second Edition (1994)
Joycelyn M. Pollock-Byrne, University of Houston–Downtown

It's About Time: America's Imprisonment Binge (1994)
John Irwin, Professor Emeritus, San Francisco State University
James Austin, National Council on Crime and Delinquency

Sense and Nonsense about Crime and Drugs: A Policy Guide, Third Edition (1994)
Samuel Walker, University of Nebraska at Omaha

It's About Time America's Imprisonment Binge

JOHN IRWIN
Professor Emeritus, San Francisco State University

JAMES AUSTIN
National Council on Crime and Delinquency

Wadsworth Publishing Company
Belmont, California
A Division of Wadsworth, Inc.

Criminal Justice Editor: Brian Gore
Editorial Assistant: Jennifer Dunning
Production Coordinator: Debby Kramer
Production Editor: Merrill Peterson
Print Buyer: Karen Hunt
Permissions Editor: Jeanne Bosschart
Designer: Andrew Ogus
Copy Editor: Victoria Nelson
Cover: Stephen Rapley
Compositor: T:H Typecast, Inc.
Printer: Malloy Lithographing

This book is printed on acid-free recycled paper.

International Thomson Publishing
The trademark ITP is used under license

Printed in the United States of America

2 3 4 5 6 7 8 9 10 — 97 96 95 94

Library of Congress Cataloging-in-Publication Data

Irwin, John, 1929–
It's about time : America's imprisonment binge / John Irwin and James Austin.
p. cm.—(Contemporary issues in crime and justice series)
Includes index.
ISBN 0-534-21906-3
1. Prisons—United States. 2. Imprisonment—United States.
3. Corrections—United States. I. Austin, James, 1948–
II. Title. III. Series.
HV9471.I774 1993
365'.973—dc20 93-25165

ISBN 0-534-21906-3

Dedicated to the hundreds
of people who have not given up
the struggle to make our criminal justice
system fair, rational and humane

Contents

Foreword

The Contemporary Issues in Crime and Justice Series introduces important topics that until now have been neglected or inadequately covered to students and professionals in criminal justice, criminology, sociology, and related fields. The volumes cover philosophical and theoretical issues and analyze the most recent research findings and their implications for practice. Each volume is intended to stimulate further thinking and debate on its subject as well as provide direction for policy formulation and implementation.

In this stimulating treatise on America's "imprisonment binge," Irwin and Austin forcefully argue that we must turn away from excessive use of prisons as the answer to the nation's "crime problem." Citing figures that we now imprison at a higher rate than any nation in the world (including South Africa) and the fact that young African-American and Hispanic males are widely overrepresented in prisons and jails, they suggest that our current approach to sentencing and dealing with crime is in need of critical review. Throughout this work, the authors take an insightful look into how we have arrived at imprisonment as the primary solution to our crime problem. Even though we have become more punitive than at any other time in our history, they emphasize, the public still believes that America is soft on crime and wants legislators and the courts to get even "tougher" on crime.

Through careful documentation, including official crime statistics, and ethnographic studies of offenders sentenced to prison in four states, the authors take a revealing look at who goes to prison. They discover that the vast majority are admitted either for nonviolent crime or for no crimes at all (i.e., parole or technical violations). In other words, most crimes committed by those who are admitted to prison are much less severe than is popularly believed. The authors further document the disturbing trend that growing numbers of inmates leave prison in a "socially crippled and profoundly alienated" condition. Over 95 percent of these inmates are released into society, and it is likely that their problems will become even more severe over time. Another important factor in high incarceration rates is their budgetary impact on society. From the figures presented for building and operating prisons and jails, it becomes clear that our state economies, and thus important social and educational programs, are being devastated by the drainage of funds that must be expended on the corrections industry.

In the final analysis, Irwin and Austin argue that the "grand imprisonment experiment" that has dominated this country's crime reduction policy for the past two decades has failed miserably and should be abandoned. The first step in the process is to recognize that social and economic factors have a much greater impact on crime control than imprisonment. The authors argue that by substantially shortening prison terms for *most* inmates, prison overcrowding will be significantly reduced while not adversely affecting public safety. The saved money and lives could be more wisely reinvested elsewhere in the community, thereby holding the real possibility of reducing crime. While this may appear to be a rather limited recommendation for "reform," the authors make a strong argument that if we are to make any progress in this area, we must realistically assess what can be accomplished. Policy makers, educators, and the public will find this a groundbreaking work in its arguments to put an end to America's current imprisonment policies.

Roy Roberg

Preface

For the last ten years, we have been witnessing the national tragedy and disgrace of America's imprisonment binge. We, as sociologists/criminologists, have kept in close contact with America's "prison systems," including their administrators, staffs, policy makers, and, most of all, clients—the prisoners. During the 1980s, we nervously listened to our political leaders (both Republicans and Democrats) and special interest groups advocate their simplistic but appealing message that in order to solve the crime problem we needed to escalate the use of imprisonment. We were equally dismayed to witness many of our colleagues pursue government financed studies that would justify the conservative "war on crime" agenda. Then, we watched, incredulously, the unparalleled explosion of the prison populations.

Our education and experience regarding the relationship between crime and imprisonment had taught us that the set of ideas that were the conceptual building blocks of the conservative rhetoric on crime and its control were fallacious. The basic tenets of this political agenda can be summarized as follows:

- The War on Poverty, that sought to fight crime through education, job training, and rehabilitation tried in the 1960s and 1970s, was a total failure;
- Dangerous criminals repeatedly go free because of liberal judges or decisions made by the liberal Supreme Court that help the criminal, but not the victim;
- Swift and certain punishment in the form of more and longer prison terms will reduce crime by incapacitating the hardened criminals and making potential law breakers think twice before they commit crimes;
- Most inmates are dangerous and cannot be safely placed in the community;
- It will be far cheaper to society in the long run to increase the use of imprisonment;
- Greater use of imprisonment since the 1980s has in fact reduced crime;

It became increasingly apparent that nothing was working to dispel the conservative rhetoric on crime and that the prison populations were going to grow forever, or at least until the society created a veritable disaster. We, therefore, began conducting (privately financed) research to counter what we view as grossly misleading and often fallacious statements.

We first presented these in a series of pamphlets—*It's About Time, Who Goes to Prison,* and *Does Imprisonment Reduce Crime?,* which were published and distributed by the National Council on Crime and Delinquency (NCCD) over a period of five years. It is apparent that the appeal of the conservative rhetoric to the public and the size of prison populations have not been reduced by our efforts or those of other critics of current criminal justice policies. However, there are glimmers of hope. Attorney General Janet Reno and many politicians have finally begun to openly question the wisdom of lengthy mandatory prison terms for drug users. The huge costs of the imprisonment binge has led many states to abandon prison construction programs. Governors and mayors openly state that they cannot afford to build another jail or prison. Some jurisdictions are reducing their prison terms and funding alternatives to prison.

More importantly, we still believe that one of the unique attributes of American democracy is its value of diversity—both in its citizenry but also in its ideas. For a democracy to exist there must exist a marketplace of ideas that often compete with one another. The current and dominant "imprisonment reduces crime" ideology has held a stranglehold on criminal justice policy. Studies designed to objectively evaluate the effects of the conservative policy or to look at alternatives were not requested or were denied funding. For these reasons, we felt it important that an alternative perspective be articulated—a perspective that we deeply believe will ultimately become accepted. So, we wrote this book.

Admittedly, we (like most social scientists) started off with a particular purpose, but the arguments and the analysis are honest and they emerge directly from all the information and evidence we could accumulate.

Many persons and organizations helped us finish the book. Over the course of our research financial assistance was periodically provided by the Edna McConnel Clark Foundation, the Jessie Ball duPont Religious, Charitable and Educational Fund, and the NCCD.

Chase Reveland, Michael Lane, Harry Singletary, and George Sumner, all of whom were directors of state prison systems at the time of our research, granted us permission and provided us with the necessary resources to conduct our inmate interviews in Washington, Nevada, Illinois, and Florida. (Their level of support was in marked contrast to the California Department of Corrections' James Rowland who steadfastly denied us access to the nation's largest prison system.) In all four states, a number of prison guards and administrative staff, too many to mention here, assisted us in compiling inmate record data and providing access to the inmates. But in particular, we would like to thank Nola Joyce, Bill Bales, Glenn Whorton, Robin Bates, and J. W. Fairman for their assistance.

Nancy Strachan and Indy den Daas assisted in conducting many interviews of prisoners. Aaron David McVey and Bill Elms performed the state by state quantitative analysis of crime and incarceration rates. Lynne Watson edited a draft of the almost completed manuscript.

Laura Chin and Paulina Begliomini provided all the clerical and word processing assistance we needed. Roy Roberg and Barry Krisberg offered many useful suggestions for modifying earlier drafts of the manuscript. We are grateful for suggestions made by the reviewers: Dr. Bernard McCarthy, University of Central Florida; Dr. Paul Friday, Research and Training Specialists; and Edward J. Latessa, University of Cincinnati.

Finally, we want to express our deep appreciation to the more than 300 inmates and parolees we interviewed and met in the course of doing this research. Although they represent a tiny subsample of the millions of Americans who are imprisoned each year, we hope that their life experiences, as represented in this book, will lead to a more enlightened and humane imprisonment policy.

1

Our Imprisonment Binge

AMERICA'S GROWING CORRECTIONAL INDUSTRIAL COMPLEX

The United States has been engaged in an unprecedented imprisonment binge. Between 1980 and 1992, the prison population has more than doubled, from 329,821 to 883,593—a rise of 168 percent. The increase was so great that by 1991, the number of citizens incarcerated exceeded the population of six states and was larger than that of some of our major cities, including San Francisco, Washington, D.C., or Boston. The incarceration rate (number of persons in prison on any given day per 100,000 population) increased during the same time period from 138 to 329, as compared to only 26 in 1850 (Figure 1-1).[1] We now imprison at a higher rate than any nation in the world, having recently surpassed South Africa.

And there is little evidence that America's imprisonment campaign will end soon. The National Council on Crime and Delinquency (NCCD) forecasts that under the present criminal justice policies, the nation's prison population will reach 1 million inmates by 1994.[2] In 1991, 42 states reported that they were planning to build over 100,000 prison beds at a cost of over $5 billion. Yet even this massive construction program represents a futile effort to catch up with the increasing prison populations.

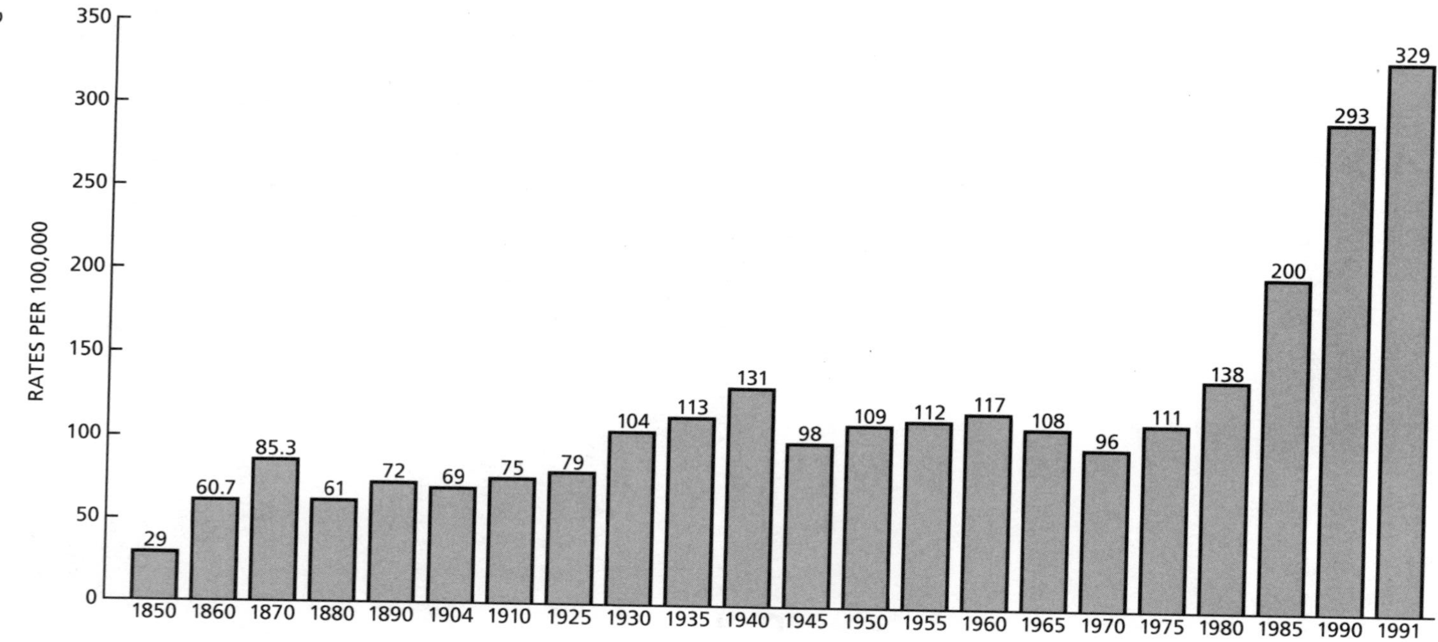

Source: Margaret Werner Cahalan, *Historical Corrections Statistics in the United States, 1850–1984*. Rockville, MD: Westat, Inc., 1986, Bureau of Justice Statistics, *Sourcebook of Criminal Justice Statistics, 1991*. Washington, D.C.: U.S. Department of Justice, 1992, and Bureau of Justice Statistics, *Prisoners in 1991*. Washington, D.C.: U.S. Department of Justice, 1992.

FIGURE 1-1 Incarceration Rates, 1850–1991

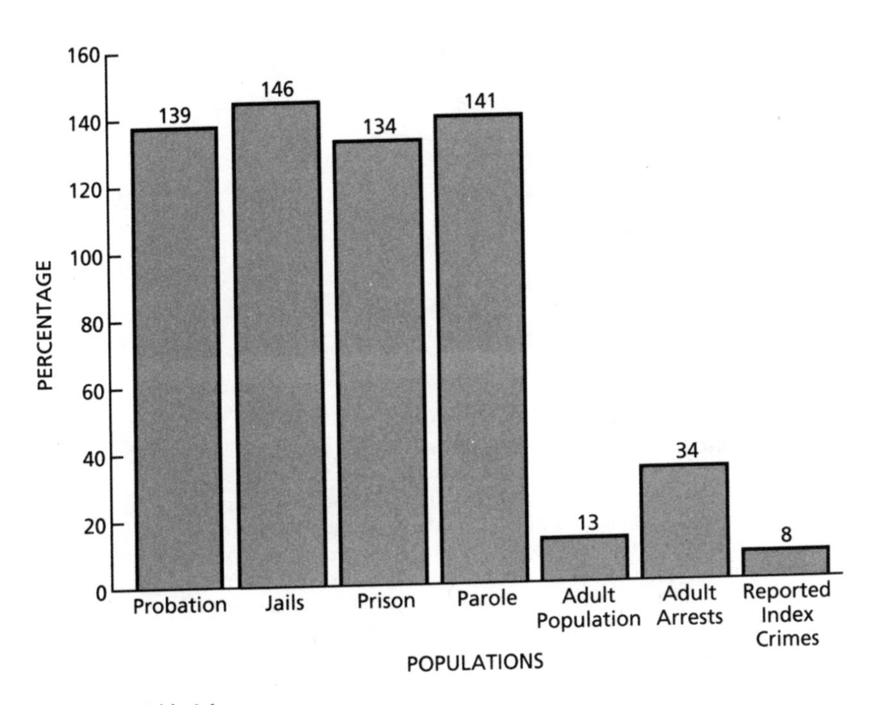

Source: See Table 1-1.

FIGURE 1-2 Percent Change in Correction Populations, 1980–1990

The rise in prison populations has been accompanied by large increases in other forms of correctional supervision. Between 1980 and 1990, the probation, parole, and jail populations (facilities that typically house pretrial defendants and offenders sentenced to short jail terms of one year or less) grew almost as rapidly as the prison population (Figure 1-2, Table 1-1). In total, 4.1 million adults—about one out of every 46—were under some form of correctional supervision. This is more than twice the rate of correctional control that existed in 1980.

Probation grew by 126 percent in this same decade and remains the dominant form of correctional supervision, with over 2.3 million adults on probation on any given day in 1990. However, more Americans experience jail time than any other form of correctional control. In 1988, the U.S. Department of Justice reported over 9.7 million

TABLE 1-1 Correction Populations
Percent Change 1980–1990

	1980	1990	% Change
Probation	1,118,097	2,670,234	139
Jails	163,994	403,019	146
Prison	329,821	771,243	134
Parole	220,438	531,407	141
Totals	1,832,350	4,375,903	139
Adult population	162.8 million	184.7 million	13
Adult arrests	6.1 million	8.2 million	34
Reported index crimes	13.4 million	14.5 million	8

Sources: U.S. Department of Justice, Bureau of Justice Statistics, *Historical Corrections Statistics in the United States, 1850–1984;* U.S. Department of Justice, Federal Bureau of Investigation, *Uniform Crime Reports: Crime in the United States, 1980 and 1990;* U.S. Department of Justice, Bureau of Justice Statistics, *Prisoners in 1990;* U.S. Department of Justice, Bureau of Justice Statistics, *Sourcebook of Criminal Justice Statistics, 1988;* U.S. Department of Justice, Bureau of Justice Statistics, *Probation and Parole, 1990;* U.S. Department of Justice, Bureau of Justice Statistics, *Jail Inmates, 1990* (Washington, D.C.: U.S. Government Printing Office).

admissions to the nation's 3,300 plus jails. Assuming that approximately 75 percent of these 9.7 million admissions represents mutually exclusive adults, this means that nearly one out of every twenty-five adults in America go to jail each year.

Those under the control of correctional authority do not represent a cross-section of the nation's population. They tend to be young African-American and Latino males who are uneducated, without jobs, or, at best, marginally employed in low-paying jobs. According to one recent study, the average daily populations of those in prison, parole, probation, and jail revealed that:

- Almost one in four (23 percent) African-American men in the age group 20–29 is either in prison, jail, probation, or parole on any given day.
- Sixty years ago, less than one-fourth of prison admissions were nonwhite. Today, nearly half are nonwhite.

- Over one out of every ten Hispanic men (10.4 percent) in the same age group is either in prison, jail, probation, or parole on any given day.
- For white men the ratio is considerably lower—one in 16 (or 6.2 percent).
- The number of young African-American men under control of the criminal justice system (609,690) is greater than the total number of African-American men of all ages enrolled in college as of 1986 (436,000).[3]

THE POLITICS OF THE FEAR OF CRIME

Several factors have fueled the imprisonment binge. The most powerful has been the public's growing fear of crime. This fear was initially aroused by a substantial increase in the major "index" crimes (homicides, assaults, robberies, rape, burglary, theft, and arson) reported to police in the late 1960s and early 1970s. The public has continued to believe that crime has been increasing, and their fear of crime has remained high. Moreover, the public remains pessimistic that crime, unlike other social issues, can be reduced. A recent national poll found that only 31 percent of Americans believe that crime will decline in the near future (Table 1-2).[4]

Through the 1980s, the fear of crime and drug abuse was elevated each election year by the attention that politicians and the media give to crime and drug problems. As shown in Figure 1-3, the public's attention accelerated dramatically at the end of this decade. As we suggested in an earlier publication:

> Politicians harangue on the *street crime* problem because it is a safe issue. It is easy to cast in simple terms of good versus evil and no powerful constituency is directly offended by a campaign against street crime. Some politicians also use street crime to divert attention away from other pressing social problems—such as the threat of nuclear war, unemployment, high living costs and the economy—all of which persistently top the list of public

TABLE 1-2 Public Attitudes on Key Social Issues

Question	Percent Optimistic	Pessimistic	Not Sure
1. Crime will decrease	31	66	3
2. Health care problems will be solved	32	65	3
3. Education will improve	61	37	2
4. Environment will improve	61	37	2
5. More Americans who want work will find it	68	30	2

Source: Gannett News Service poll conducted December 10–15, 1992, by Louis Harris and Associates by telephone among 1,005 registered voters. Margin of error is plus or minus 3 percentage points.

> concerns. Measures to solve these problems would require changes that would offend powerful interest groups.[5]

Marsha Rosenbaum, in her analysis of the nation's War on Drugs, pointed out that the drug problem has received similar treatment:

> The Reagan administration initiated a "War on Drugs" in the early 1980's. The Bush administration appointed a "Drug Czar," and recently offered a major plan to remove the "scourge" of drugs from the American landscape. The media have reported on the violence occurring in our inner cities and in cocaine-source nations like Colombia. The public is bombarded with news about drugs, like the drug death of sports figure Len Bias and the confessions of celebrities about personal struggles with substance abuse.[6]

The War on Drugs also spurred a movement toward more punitive sentencing policies for drug offenders. In addition, mandatory drug testing and a reduction in affordable publicly funded drug treatment programs has meant that more and more released felons are being returned to prison for use of illegal drugs.[7] Moreover, because this war is focused on crack cocaine, which is mainly sold and used in inner city communities, it is increasing the already disproportionately

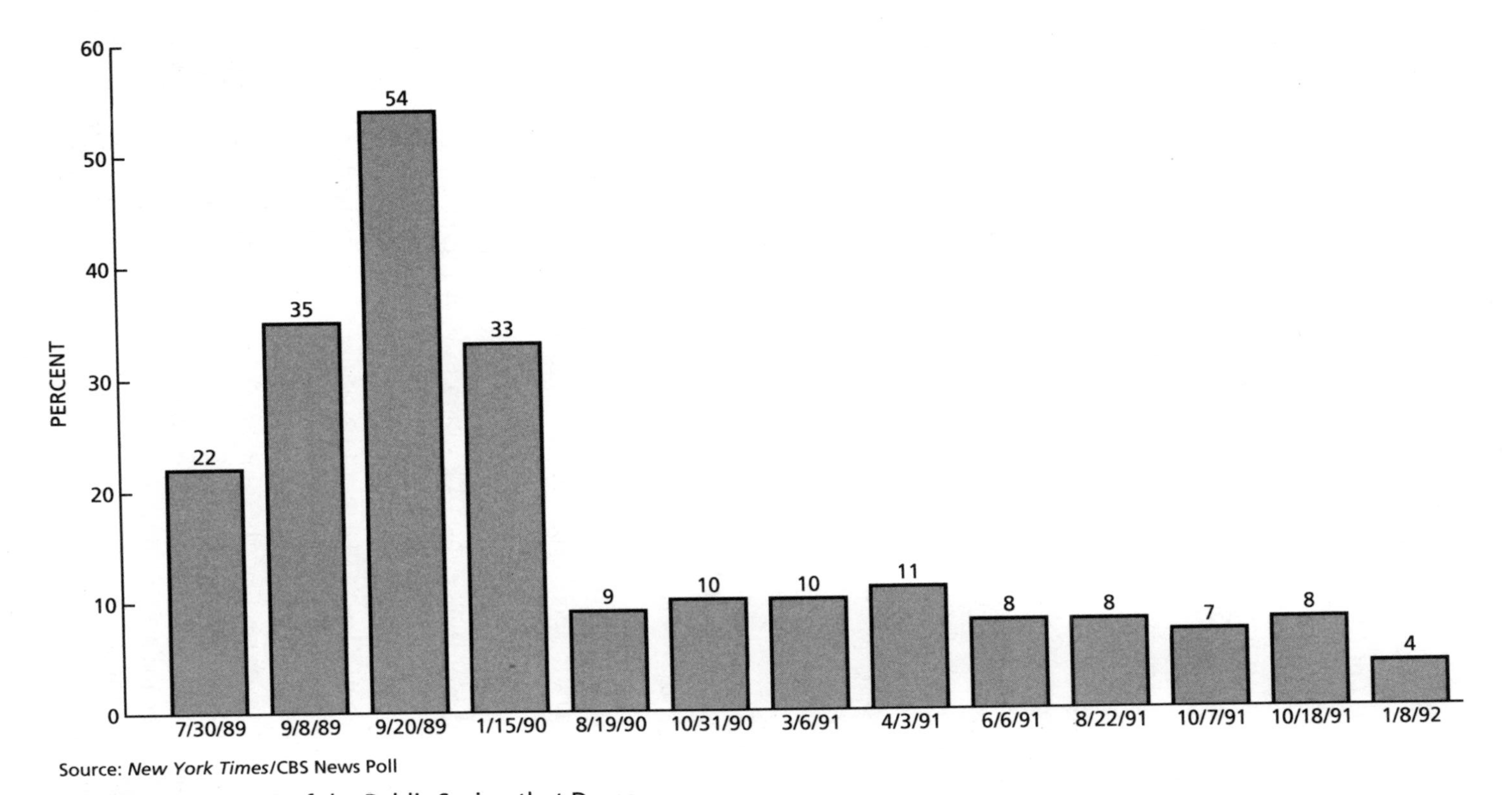

Source: *New York Times*/CBS News Poll

FIGURE 1-3 Percent of the Public Saying that Drugs Are the Most Important Problem Facing the U.S.A.

high number of African-American and Hispanic prisoners. For example, in 1926, the first year that the race of prison admissions was recorded on a national basis, only 21 percent of all prison admissions were African American. By 1970, that figure had increased to 39 percent; by 1989, it had further grown to 46 percent.[8]

In their steady and unrelenting harangues on the crime and drug problems, politicians have argued that steady and dramatic expansion of prison populations is absolutely necessary to maintain a safe society. They argue that massive increases in imprisonment are positive signs —indications that the nation is increasingly intolerant of criminals and their antisocial and too often violent behavior. Moreover, they claim that increasing the use of imprisonment in particular and punishment in general has reduced crime. Former Attorney General William Barr recently restated this position well, indicating that the country had a "clear choice": either to build more prisons or to tolerate higher violent crime rates.[9]

AMERICA'S HISTORY OF WAREHOUSING PRISONERS

Imprisonment as society's punishment for serious crime has been part of the American social fabric since the founding of this country. In colonial times, before the American Revolution, most felons were fined, whipped, branded, publicly shamed, or banished. A few were executed. The prison, a special location in which to place people for punishment for their crimes, was introduced soon after the revolution, ostensibly as a device to reform offenders. Americans, rejecting what they saw as excessively cruel measures employed in England and in the colonies under English rule, adopted the concept of the "penitentiary," where felons would "be kept in quiet solitude, reflecting penitently on their sins in order that they might cleanse and transform themselves."[10] After several decades of building and running penitentiaries, the states more or less gave up on reformation but continued to use the prison as the main form of punishment for serious crime.

During the nineteenth century, prisons became extremely cruel places in which convicts were kept under control through brutal forms of corporal punishment and were frequently used as cheap labor.

Around 1900, federal legislation and emerging union power forced most convict labor out of the public sector. For the next 50 years, prisons were "big houses"—fortresslike institutions where prisoners did little more than "time." After World War II, many states returned to the reformative goal, with some new social scientific embellishments. Prisoners were to be "rehabilitated" through new scientific methods. This era lasted until it was decided that rehabilitative efforts appeared to make little difference and prisons (like society in general) entered into a conservative and punitive period, which continues today. Now felons are sent to prison to receive their "just desserts" and to be deterred from committing crimes in the future.

In examining this history of shifting rationales for imprisonment, it becomes clear that none of them accounts for our persistent and almost exclusive reliance on prison as the appropriate response to serious crime. What does explain it is the American people's strong desire to banish from their midst any population of people who are threatening, bothersome, and repulsive. As David Rothman points out in *The Discovery of the Asylum,* this is what was done from the outset with the insane, the feeble minded, the poor, wayward children, and felons.[11] We continue to do it with the elderly poor, troublesome insane, street rabble, and felons.[12]

The pattern is particularly clear in the latest upsurge in the use of the prison, which followed a period (1965–1970) during which there was considerable interest in finding other forms of punishment and actual success in significantly lowering prison populations. Since that time, however, many unsettling developments have made Americans more fearful, conservative, and mean spirited. The aforementioned perception of steady increases in crime is one contributing factor. But more fundamental are nationwide economic difficulties. Soaring inflation, high unemployment, and a decline in real wages of a significant proportion of the middle class have caused uncertainty about the economic future. Also, the proliferation of materialistic, ostentatious parvenus (e.g., Donald Trump) and the expansion of an underclass perceived as menacing have offended the public. These disturbing developments have been aggravated by the perception that, because of global, unmanageable economic processes, our society's economic problems are insoluble.

In terms of reducing our crime rate or in reducing the size and costs of corrections, the following social and economic trends offer little reason for optimism for the future:

- Between 1980 and 1988, the number of persons living in poverty increased from 26 million to 32 million (23 percent increase).
- There are 12.5 million children, or nearly one out of every five children, living in poverty.
- For minority children, the figures are even more desperate: one out of every two African-American children and one out of every three Hispanic children live in poverty.
- The number of single-parent families, predominantly headed by females, increased from 22 percent in 1980 to 27 percent by 1987.
- The United States ranks 20th out of 22 industrialized countries in infant mortality rates.
- Since 1970, the number of one-parent families has nearly tripled to more than 10.1 million. About 29 percent of the 35 million families in 1990 have only one parent.
- From 35 to 40 million Americans lack medical insurance.

Why are these disturbing trends emerging now? Part of the explanation lies in fundamental shifts in the distribution of wealth, as documented by Kevin Phillips in his recent book, *The Politics of Rich and Poor.*[13] Phillips, using a wide variety of official data, argues that the government economic policies of the past decade have improved the economic status of the rich at the expense of the lower and middle classes. Some of the more striking economic trends he identifies are the following:

- In 1987, the income of the typical African-American family ($18,098) equaled just 56.1 percent of the typical white family's income, the lowest comparative ratio since the 1960s.
- Between 1979 and 1987, earnings for male high school graduates with one to five years of work experience declined by 18 percent.
- Between 1981 and 1987, the nation lost over 1 million manufacturing jobs.
- Between 1977 and 1988, the average after-tax family income of the lowest 10 percent, in current dollars, fell from $3,528 to $3,157 (a 10.5 percent decline). Conversely, the income of the

top 10 percent increased from $70,459 to $89,783 (a 24.4 percent increase) and the incomes of the top 1 percent increased from $174,498 to $303,900 (a 74 percent increase).

- Between 1981 and 1988, the total compensation of chief executives increased from $373,000 to $773,000 (an increase of 107 percent), and the number of millionaires and billionaires increased by more than 250 percent.[14]

In economic terms, America is becoming a more fragmented and segregated society. These trends not only contribute to crime rates and other social problems, but also fuel a growing public demand to fund criminal justice services. In particular, the number of those Americans who are uneducated and raised in impoverished conditions will continue to grow and justify the need to further expand the correctional system. As Phillips states:

> For women, young people, and minorities the effect of economic polarization during the 1980's was largely negative. The nation as a whole also suffered as unemployable young people drove up the crime rate and expanded the drug trade. Broken families and unwed teenage mothers promised further welfare generations and expense. And none of it augured well for the future skills level and competitiveness of the U.S. work force.[15]

Our society faces an enormous public policy dilemma. On one hand we are expending a greater portion of our public dollars on incarcerating, punishing, treating, and controlling persons who are primarily from the lower economic classes in an effort to reduce crime. On the other hand, we have set in motion economic policies that serve to widen the gap between the rich and the poor, producing yet another generation of impoverished youths who will probably end up under the control of the correctional system. By escalating the size of the correctional system, we are also increasing the tax burden and diverting billions of dollars from those very public services (education, health, transportation, and economic development) that would reduce poverty, unemployment, crime, drug abuse, and mental illness.[16] Although we have become more punitive than at any other time in our history, the public still believes that America is soft on crime and wants legislators and the courts to "get tougher" on crime, especially in the face of what they believe are rising crime rates and a declining standard of living.

In many ways, our current situation is similar to that of eighteenth-century England, which was passing through even more unsettling changes than we are today and was faced with unprecedented crime waves in its new, crowded, filthy, polluted, slum encircled, rabble-ridden cities.[17] After experimenting with extraordinary punishments, particularly wholesale hanging and the use of prison barges, England turned to banishment as its primary penal measure. An important difference between eighteenth-century England and modern-day America, however, is that the world offered England locations to which it could send its felons—first America and then Australia. Between 1787 and 1868, hundreds of thousands of convicts (over 100,000 in the first fleet) were transported to Australia.

America has had to construct its locations of banishment within its borders. This it is doing at a feverish pace. As was done in eighteenth-century England, we are now using barges in New York City. Although we lack an Australia where we can set up prison colonies, we are increasingly building huge megaprison settlements in isolated rural locations where land is cheap and recession-starved communities are anxious for the economic benefits that a major prison will bring.

WHAT HAS BEEN ACCOMPLISHED BY THE IMPRISONMENT BINGE?

Americans want several things accomplished by their support of our expensive imprisonment practices. Above all, they want to feel safer in their homes, in their neighborhoods, on the street, or in any public place. For this reason, they want menacing "street criminals" removed and placed in prison. They are also angry at criminals, particularly the types highlighted in the media and by politicians—people such as Willie Horton, the convict who committed a rape while on work furlough and became a campaign issue in the Bush-Dukakis presidential election—and they want these hard-case felons to receive appropriate punishment for their crimes. Moreover, they want apprehended criminals punished harshly so that other potential or active criminals will "think twice" before committing a crime in the future. Finally, they want prisoners in prison to be given treatment and services that will result in their rehabilitation.[18]

Given the public perception of the crime problem, these are reasonable goals. But is the public perception of the crime problem correct? Are persons sent to prison being given appropriate punishment for their crimes? Are potential criminals deterred by imprisonment? Are prisoners having their chances of returning to crime reduced by any programs or activities that occur in our new prisons? The evidence suggests otherwise. In Chapter 6, we will address this question in much greater detail. For now, suffice it to say that most Americans agree that our crime problem has not been solved or even improved by the rise in imprisonment. If incarceration ever had a public safety benefit, it has apparently run its course.

THE COSTS OF THE IMPRISONMENT BINGE

Even though the crime rate has not gone down, the costs of punishment have skyrocketed. From 1979 to 1991, the number of criminal justice employees increased 50 percent. The largest growth was for correctional staff, who increased 104 percent. Absolute spending on corrections has increased by 217 percent, far outstripping any other segment of the criminal justice system (Figures 1-4 and 1-5). As of 1990, we were spending approximately $74 billion each year to operate the nation's entire criminal justice system. Of the $74 billion, $25 billion is spent on corrections, with 85 percent of corrections spent on jails and prisons (Figure 1-6).[19] During this past decade, state spending in corrections was the fastest-growing category of all state spending categories (Table 1-3).

Significantly, the costs of crimes to victims is far below the costs of criminal justice. In 1990, the total costs of crimes to victims as reported in the U.S. Department of Justice's National Crime Victim Survey (NCVS), was $19.2 billion, or about $560 per crime; the majority of crimes had value losses below $100. These costs include economic losses from property theft or damage, cash losses, medical expenses, loss of pay caused by victimization, and other related costs. This figure, however, does not include the reimbursement of such

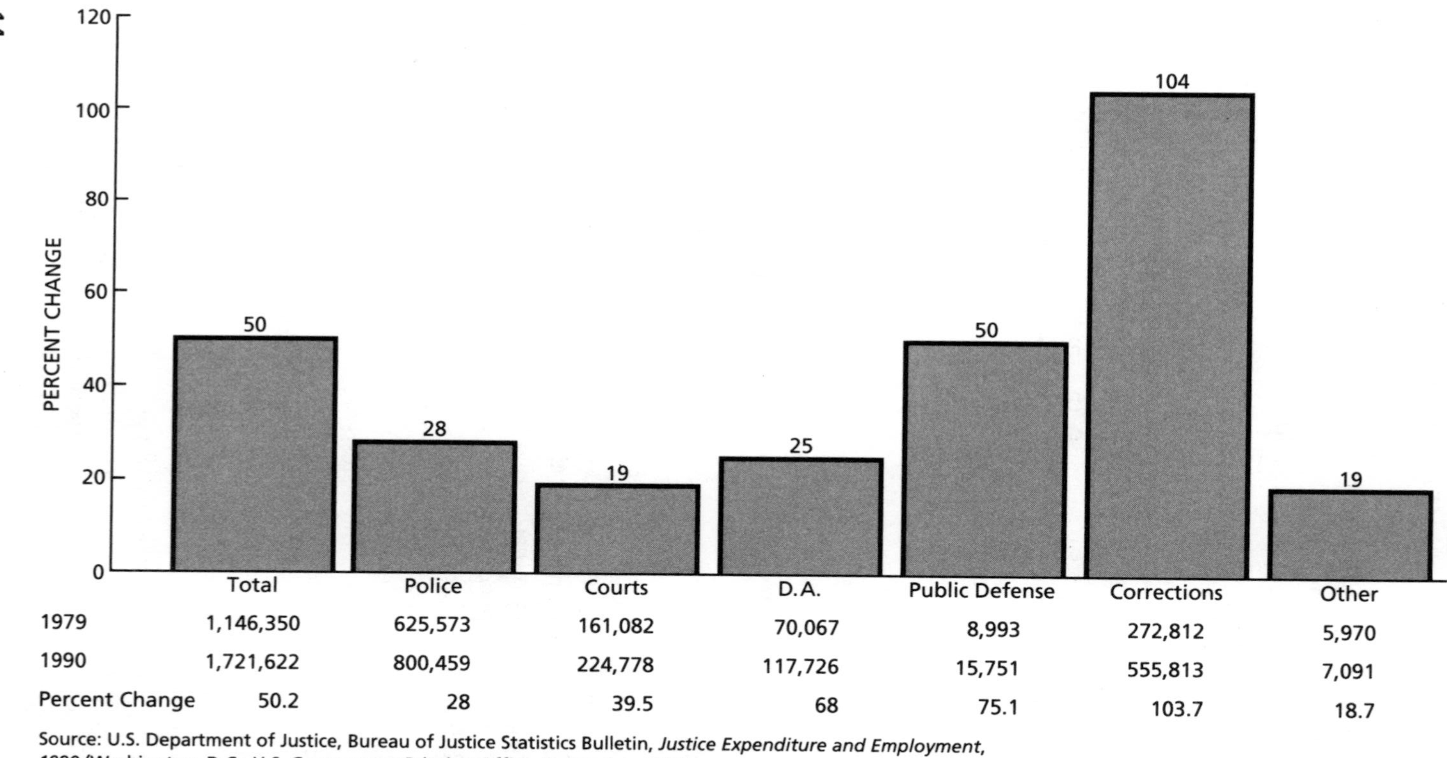

	Total	Police	Courts	D.A.	Public Defense	Corrections	Other
1979	1,146,350	625,573	161,082	70,067	8,993	272,812	5,970
1990	1,721,622	800,459	224,778	117,726	15,751	555,813	7,091
Percent Change	50.2	28	39.5	68	75.1	103.7	18.7

Source: U.S. Department of Justice, Bureau of Justice Statistics Bulletin, *Justice Expenditure and Employment, 1990* (Washington, D.C.: U.S. Government Printing Office, September 1992).

FIGURE 1-4 Percent Changes in the Number of Criminal Justice Employees, 1979–1990

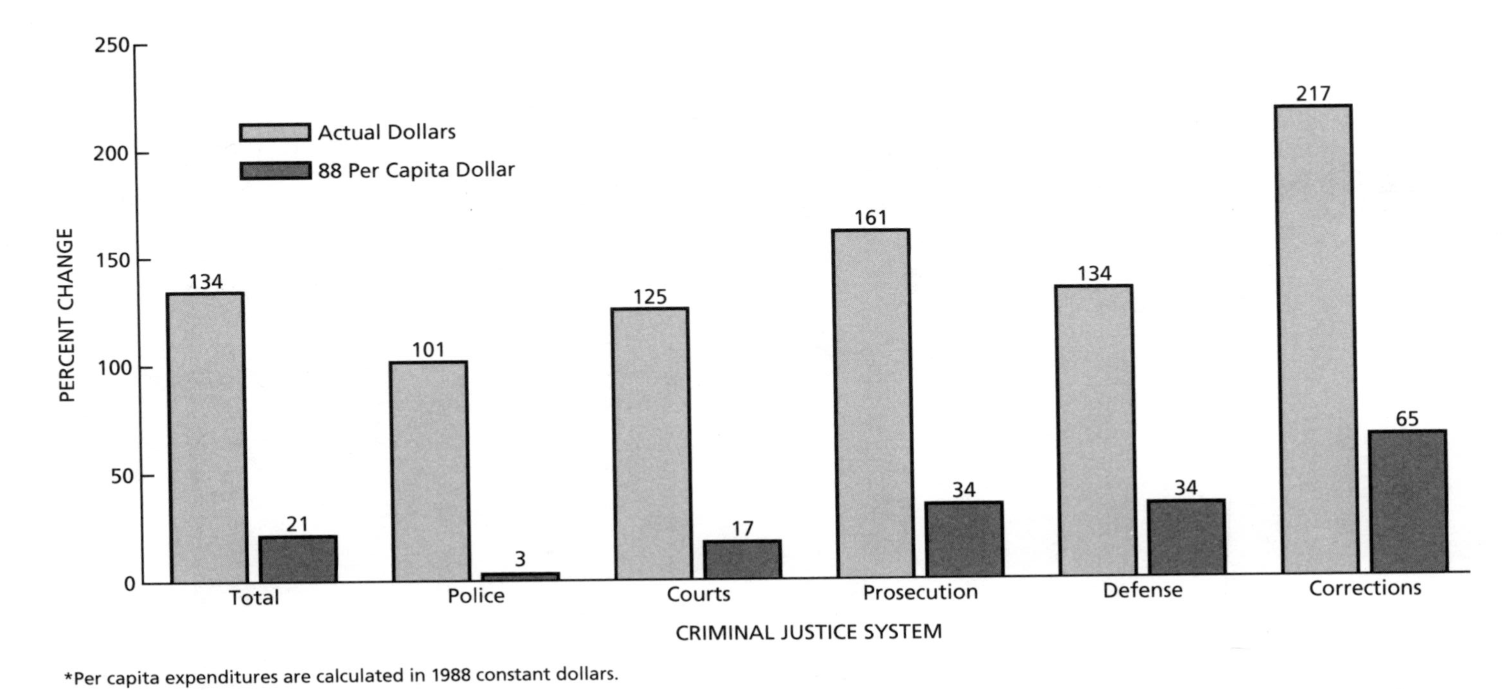

*Per capita expenditures are calculated in 1988 constant dollars.

Source: U.S. Department of Justice, Bureau of Justice Statistics Bulletin, *Justice Expenditure and Employment, 1988* (Washington, D.C.: U.S. Government Printing Office, July 1990).

FIGURE 1-5 Percent Changes in Direct Government and 1988 Per Capita Expenditures* for the Criminal Justice System 1979–1988

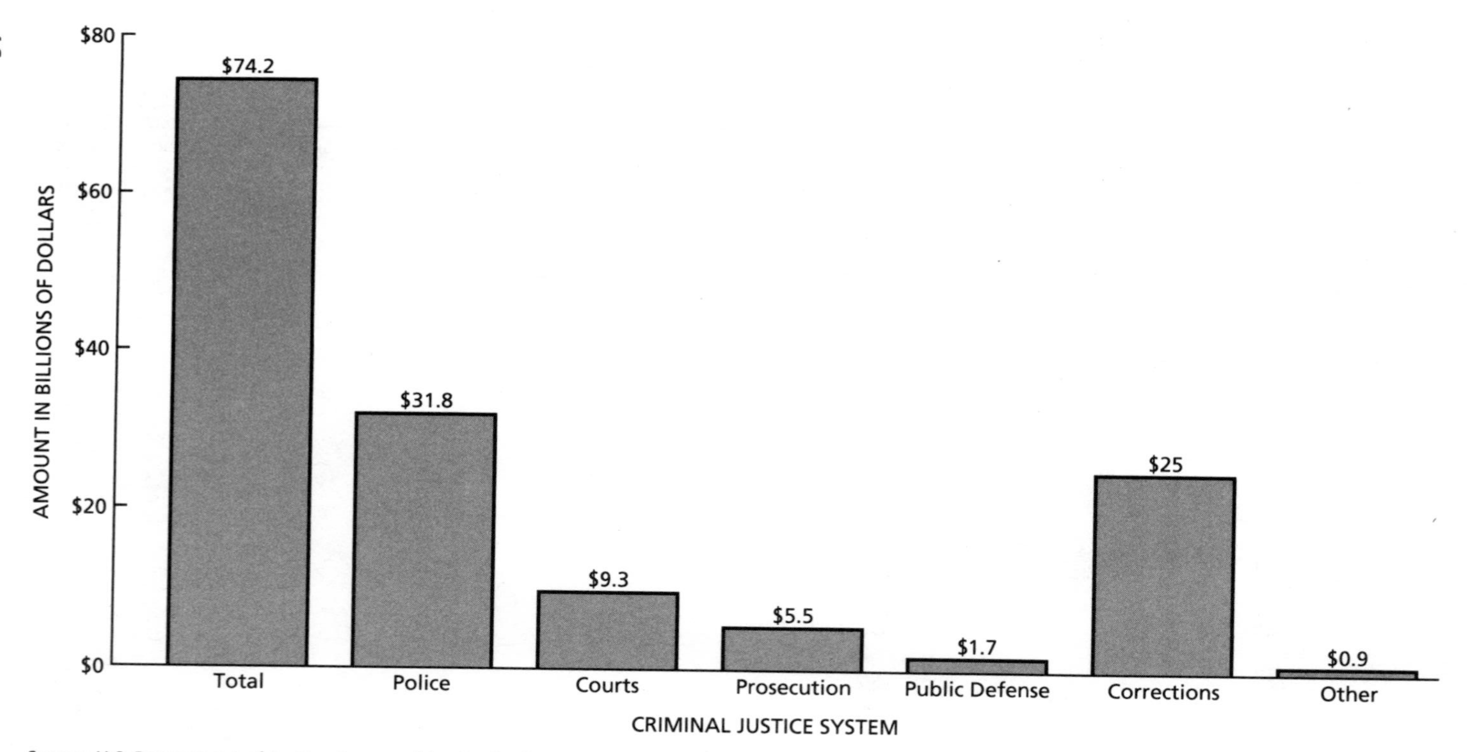

Source: U.S. Department of Justice, Bureau of Justice Statistics, *Justice Expenditure and Employment, 1990* (Washington, D.C.: U.S. Government Printing Office, September 1992).

FIGURE 1-6 Criminal Justice System Costs, 1990

TABLE 1-3 Trends in State Spending, 1980–1988*

Spending Category	1980	1988	Percent Change
Corrections	$.22	$.35	+59
Medicaid	.45	.60	+33
Health and hospitals	.60	.62	+ 3
Elementary-secondary education	2.37	2.32	− 2
Higher education	.94	.91	− 3
Highways	.74	.66	−11
Welfare (non-Medicare)	.51	.37	−27

* Spending figures reflect state spending per $100 of personal income.

Source: Steve Gold, Center for the Study of the States, Nelson A. Rockefeller Institute of Government, 1990.

losses by insurance companies or recovery by criminal justice agencies of stolen property. That recovery rate was estimated at 35 percent in 1986, which reduces the direct losses to $12.5 billion.

Given the enormous costs of aggressive imprisonment and its doubtful effectiveness on crime, one must question the wisdom of our current sentencing policies. More important, why is this draconian experiment failing so miserably? The answer lies in a better understanding of those being punished. We will examine these people in the next five chapters. We will closely observe who is going to prison today, and what happens to them in prison and immediately after their release. Then we will look at the other issues—the question of deterrence as well as the other costs, financial and social, of our imprisonment binge.

NOTES

1. U.S. Department of Justice, Bureau of Justice Statistics, *Prisoners in 1991* (Washington, D.C.: U.S. Government Printing Office, May 1992).
2. James Austin, Aaron McVey, and Michael Jones, *The Impact of Declining Drug Arrests: The 1991 NCCD Prison Population Projection* (San Francisco, Calif.: National Council on Crime and Delinquency, 1992).

3. Marc Mauer, *Americans Behind Bars: A Comparison of International Rates of Incarceration* (Washington, D.C.: The Sentencing Project, January 1991).

4. Between 1972 and 1992, the monthly Gallup Poll has shown that about half of the American public believes that crime is increasing and only 20 percent believe it has been declining (George Gallup, Jr., *The Gallup Poll Monthly,* report no. 318 [Princeton, N.J.: The Gallup Poll, March 1992]). In a 1987 study in Ohio, 86 percent of the respondents answered "True" to the statement, "The crime rate has been going up steadily for the past 10 years" (Jeffrey J. Knowles, "Ohio Citizen Attitudes Concerning Crime and Criminal Justice [Ohio: Governor's Office of Criminal Justice Services, 1987]). It is also noteworthy that the public is far more accepting of the notion of alternatives to prison and jail sanctions as they learn more details about the crime, the offender, and the relative costs of alternative sanctions (John Doble and Josh Klein, *Punishing Criminals: The Public's View: An Alabama Survey* [New York: Edna McConnell Clark Foundation, 1989]).

5. John Irwin and James Austin, *It's About Time* (San Francisco, Calif.: National Council on Crime and Delinquency, 1987).

6. Marsha Rosenbaum, *Just Say What?* (San Francisco, Calif.: National Council on Crime and Delinquency, 1989), p. 1.

7. See Brandy Britton and Marsha Rosenbaum, *The Dollars and Sense of Fiscal Austerity: The Defunding and Privatization of Methadone Maintenance in the United States* (San Francisco, Calif.: Scientific Analysis Corporation, undated).

8. U.S. Department of Justice, Bureau of Justice Statistics, *Race of Prisoners Admitted to State and Federal Institutions, 1926–86* and *Sourcebook of Criminal Justice Statistics, 1989* (Washington, D.C.: U.S. Government Printing Office, 1991).

9. William P. Barr, "Expanding Capacity for Serious Offenders," Attorney General's Summit on Corrections, Ritz Carlton Hotel, McLean, Virginia, April 27, 1992.

10. John Irwin, *Prisons in Turmoil* (Boston: Little Brown, 1980), p. 2.

11. David Rothman, *The Discovery of the Asylum* (Boston: Little Brown, 1971).

12. In his study of the county jail, *The Jail,* John Irwin discovered that it was intended as a device to help manage society's rabble—disorganized and disreputable people (Berkeley, Calif.: University of California Press, 1985).
13. Kevin Phillips, *The Politics of Rich and Poor* (New York: Random House, 1991).
14. Ibid.
15. Ibid., p. 208.
16. In 1981, a Gallup poll discovered that 70 percent of Americans had no confidence in the criminal court's ability to sentence and convict criminals. More recently, a study in Alabama revealed the same lack of confidence in the courts; 69 percent agreed that Alabama needs more prisons (Doble and Klein, *Punishing Criminals*).
17. England was also experiencing its own drug problem, that of "killer gin." See Robert Hughes, *The Fatal Shore* (New York: Random House, 1988), chapter 2, for an excellent discussion of threats from crime, the urban "mobs," or the "dangerous classes" in England, which led to expansion of transportation as a remedy.
18. A recent study by John Doble of the Public Agenda Foundation found that besides wanting criminals punished and incapacitated, Americans believe that criminals are produced by remedial circumstances and want prisons to rehabilitate prisoners into peaceful and productive citizens (*Crime and Punishment: The Public's View* [New York: Edna McConnell Clark Foundation, 1987).
19. U.S. Department of Justice, Bureau of Justice Statistics, *Justice Expenditure and Employment, 1990* (Washington, D.C.: U.S. Government Printing Office, September, 1992).

2

Who Goes to Prison?

PUBLIC MISPERCEPTIONS ABOUT WHO GOES TO PRISON

The public reacts to crime with fear and intensity because they have been led to believe by the media and public officials that thousands of vicious, intractable street criminals menace innocent citizens. Actually, they have two slightly different images of the new street criminal. The "softer" version is that of a person who persists in committing property crimes even after repeated opportunities to live an honest life and after being arrested many times and serving numerous jail and prison sentences. The "harder" version is that of a violent criminal, equally intractable, who goes about his or her predatory crimes with no regard for other humans. When he snatches purses from old ladies, he bashes them in the head because he enjoys hurting people. When he robs a mom-and-pop grocery store, he executes his victims with a sneer on his face. Most Americans still believe that thousands of these two slightly different types of street criminals stalk our streets; raid our homes; rape, assault, and murder innocent citizens; and generally menace and vilify our society.

For years, criminologists debunked the "evil person" theory of crime and instead attributed the crime problem to social and economic conditions. But recently, many researchers, perhaps swayed by the general conservative shift or lured by government incentives in the form of grants, jobs, and recognition, have resurrected old theories of the "criminal type" (now most often labeled the "career criminal") and have searched for methods to identify such career criminals.

This trend started in 1970, when Marvin E. Wolfgang, Robert M. Figlio, and Thorsten Sellin examined the arrest records of all youths born in Philadelphia in 1945 and discovered that 6 percent of the youth in that "birth cohort" accounted for more than half of all the arrests or police contacts of the entire cohort.[1] The idea that a few criminals commit most of the crime—along with the hope that there was some way to identify these persons before they embarked on their criminal careers—evolved from this study.

In the early 1980s, Peter Greenwood of the Rand Corporation set out to identify "high-rate" offenders in samples of incarcerated burglars and robbers.[2] Greenwood and Alan Abrahamse asked these prisoners how much crime they had committed in the months before incarceration. Ten percent of their sample stood out from the rest in the number of crimes they reported, and a set of characteristics distinguished this subgroup of high-rate offenders from the other robbers and burglars. Even though Peter Greenwood and Susan Turner discovered later that persons identified by these same characteristics actually did not continue to commit crimes of the type and at the rate expected of high-rate offenders (a finding that caused Peter Greenwood to recant his earlier claims), the idea of the high-rate offender or career criminal had taken hold.[3]

In a series of longitudinal studies, Al Blumstein, along with various coauthors, examined different "criminal careers," which they offer as a category independent of that of career criminal.[4] (All persons who are arrested have a criminal career even if they commit one crime, which would constitute their entire criminal career.) Blumstein and his colleagues located subgroups of male offenders who, instead of maturing out of crime like the vast majority of offenders, continue to commit crime at the same rate throughout a relatively extended criminal career, that is, until they were past 35 years old. Blumstein abstained from calling these persons either high-rate offenders (actually, the frequency with which they committed crimes was relatively low) or career criminals. Blumstein recognized instead that the idea of career criminal implies something different about certain individuals that propel them toward a career in crime. This is particularly essential in employing the concept of career criminal in criminal justice decisions, because there must be some way to distinguish career criminals early in their careers from the majority of offenders who do not persist in crime.

Blumstein's "persisters," it turned out, were not identified until far along on their criminal careers, and he and his associates could not locate any "background" characteristics that separated them from many other male offenders who had less enduring criminal careers. In estimating the effect of Blumstein's articles, however, David Greenberg pointed out that there is a tendency for "laypersons to oversimplify, misunderstand, or lose sight of distinctions and qualifications criminologists make," and to see in these studies the positive identification of the career criminal. And this misperception definitely occurred, particularly among criminal justice policy makers. Characterizing the search as fruitless, Michael Gottfredson and Travis Hirschi noted:

> On March 26, 1982, 14 leading members of the criminology community in the United States met in Washington, D.C. to discuss the future of criminal justice research in this country. The priority area for future research listed first by this panel was "criminal careers." . . . Four years later, the criminal career notion so dominates discussion of criminal justice policy and so controls expenditure of federal research funds that it may now be said that criminal justice research in this country is indeed centrally planned.[5]

Fear of crime and these new images of the criminal have encouraged politicians and judges to change sentencing laws and practices, a practice that has multiplied prison populations. But are the popular images and the social scientists' ideas about contemporary criminals accurate? We think not, for the simple reason that most of these popular images of crime and criminals are shaped by the media, and media depiction consists mostly of selective attention on sensational crimes, politicians' rhetoric, and studies of career criminals funded by the federal government.

In these studies, social scientists have formed most of their ideas in "armchairs" (or now, more accurately, at computer desks), using evidence that is unreliable and skimpy—police arrest records, prison files, and convicts' penciled-in answers to questionnaires—which they study to discover the elusive traits of the career criminal. Very few of these criminologists have spent any significant time observing or talking to their subjects, the prisoners, something absolutely necessary to develop an accurate understanding of offenders' motives and criminal practices.

To discover who is actually going to prison, the extent of their criminal involvement, the seriousness of their crimes, and the "danger" they pose to society, we pursued a broad research methodology. In addition to examining the official records, we conducted lengthy interviews of persons sentenced to prison. This is not to say that we ignored the records and available statistics, but we went beyond the so-called hard data and sought a more accurate and comprehensive understanding of a complex social issue.

NATIONAL TRENDS ON PRISON ADMISSIONS

In 1990, the last year that national data are available, approximately 475,000 persons were sent to prison (Figure 2-1). Contrary to popular perceptions, the vast majority of these inmates were admitted for either nonviolent crimes or no crimes at all. About 68 percent were sentenced to prison directly from the court (new court commitments). However, a significant proportion (28 percent) were admitted for parole violations, two-thirds of which were technical violations in which a parolee was not convicted of a crime but had violated the terms of his or her parole supervision (e.g., failing a drug test, failing to appear for an office appointment, etc.).

For those who did receive a court sentence, approximately 70 percent were sentenced for nonviolent crimes. The most prevalent crimes were burglary, drugs (possession, trafficking, or conspiracy to distribute or manufacture), robbery, and public-order-related crimes (Table 2-1). The majority of new admissions were young males (ages 18–29), disproportionately African American (57 percent), and lacking a formal high school education (64 percent).

Another misperception of the public is that most persons convicted for serious crimes are infrequently imprisoned. Using national data, we can see that this perception is profoundly inaccurate (Table 2-2). According to the U.S. Department of Justice, of the 677,000

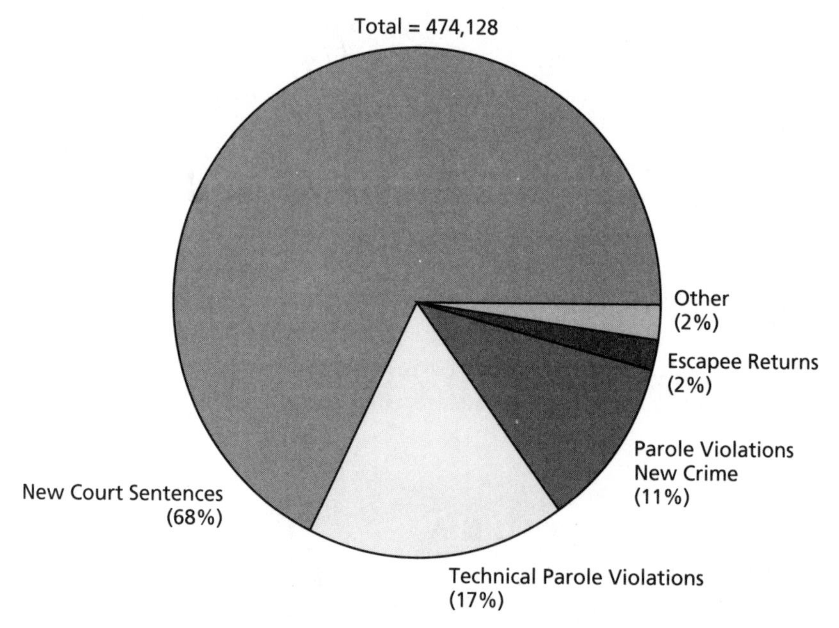

Source: U.S. Department of Justice, Bureau of Justice Statistics, Correctional Populations in the United States, 1990 (Washington, D.C.: U.S. Government Printing Office, July 1992).

FIGURE 2-1 Reasons for Being Sent to Prison, 1990

persons convicted of felony crimes in 1990, 69 percent received a sentence involving some form of incarceration, with the most frequent form of imprisonment being prison (43 percent), followed by jail (26 percent).[6] It should be emphasized that these figures exclude the millions of persons detained in jails in pretrial status who are never convicted of any crime or are put on probation. As shown in Figure 2-2, there are nearly 12.6 million admissions per year into the various correctional systems, with most admissions occurring within the nation's vast jail system (10.1 million admissions).

For those sentenced to prison, the overall average sentence length imposed by the court was 6.25 years. The U.S. Department of Justice estimates that inmates will serve an average of 25 months in prison before being released. This is an underestimate of the length of imprisonment of contemporary prisoners for at least two reasons.

First, it excludes the time prisoners have spent in jail in pretrial status awaiting the court's disposition. In most large cities, defendants

TABLE 2-1 1990 Prison Admission Characteristics

Characteristic	Percent	Characteristic	Percent
Sex		Offenses*	
Male	92.8	Violent crimes	29.9
Female	7.2	Homicide	4.9
Race		Kidnapping	0.7
White	48.5	Rape	3.0
Black	50.9	Other sex assault	3.2
Other	0.7	Robbery	10.7
Ethnicity		Assault	6.7
Hispanic	17.8	Other violent	0.6
Non-Hispanic	82.2	Property crimes	37.1
Age at admission		Burglary	17.5
Under 18 years	1.1	Larceny-theft	9.1
18–24 years	31.1	Auto theft	2.6
25–29 years	26.1	Arson	0.7
30–34 years	19.2	Fraud	4.5
35–44 years	17.0	Stolen property	2.0
45+	5.3	Other property	0.7
Median age	28 years	Drug offenses	25.1
Education		Possession	7.6
Less than 12 years	63.5	Trafficking	13.5
Median education	11th grade	Other drug	4.0
		Public Order	6.9
		Weapons	1.9
		Other public order	5.0
		Other offenses	1.0

* Based on 1988 data for 206,028 prison admissions in 35 states.

Source: BJS, *Sourcebook of Criminal Justice Statistics, 1991,* Washington, D.C.: U.S. Department of Justice, 1982.

who are eventually sentenced to prison will spend about six months in pretrial status over and above the 25-month figure. Second, this estimate is based on the length of time served by inmates in 1988 who were sentenced under pre-1988 sentencing laws. Since so many states have passed conservative sentencing laws designed to lengthen prison term by many years, length-of-stay data based on 1988 releases will be

TABLE 2-2 Dispositions of Felony Convictions, 1990

Crime	Number	Percent	Percent Prison	Percent Jail	Prison Sentence (months)	Percent Life	Prison Length of Stay (months)
Total	676,906	100	43	26	75	1	25
Murder	9,340	1	91	4	239	26	98
Rape	15,562	2	69	18	183	3	68
Robbery	37,432	6	75	14	114	1	43
Aggravated assault	37,566	6	45	27	89	.4	30
Burglary	101,050	15	54	21	74	.1	23
Larceny	95,258	14	39	26	50	0	15
Drug trafficking	111,950	17	41	30	66	.5	21
Other felonies	268,748	40	34	29	54	1	16

Source: U.S. Department of Justice, Bureau of Justice Statistics, *National Judicial Reporting Program, 1988,* (Washington, D.C.: U.S. Government Printing Office, December 1992).

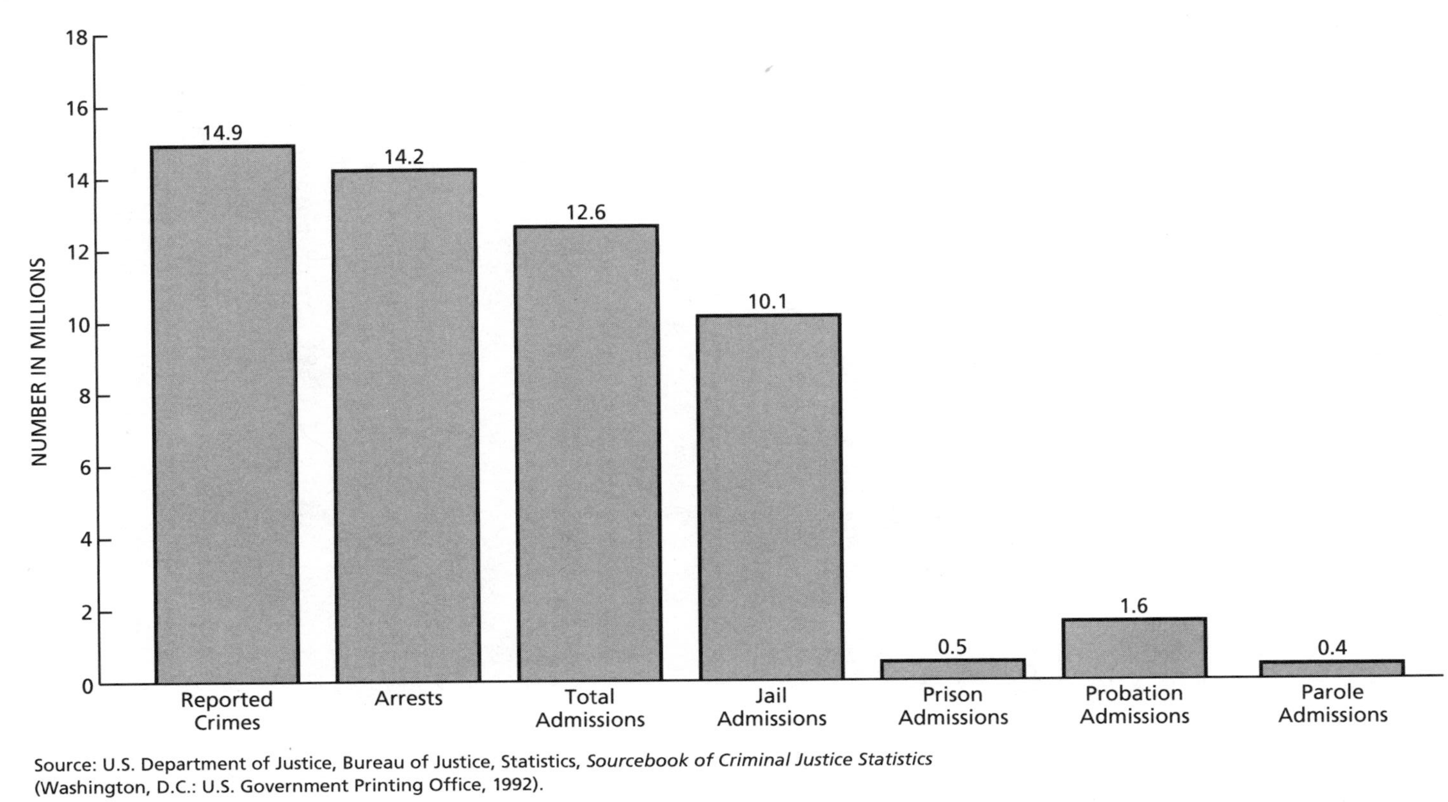

Source: U.S. Department of Justice, Bureau of Justice, Statistics, *Sourcebook of Criminal Justice Statistics* (Washington, D.C.: U.S. Government Printing Office, 1992).

FIGURE 2-2 Crimes, Arrests, and Cases Processed, 1990

inaccurate. It will be years before the effects of mandatory minimum and habitual offender laws enacted by Congress and many states begin to show up in prison release data. For example, Florida enacted a revised habitual sentencing statute in 1988.[7] That law allows the court to sentence offenders with two prior felony convictions to serve prison terms in the range of five years to life. Since this law did not begin to be used until 1989, it will be many years before these habitual offenders' length-of-stay data begin to be accounted for in national release statistics.

There are no national data on such important items as the number of prior prison terms or prior felony convictions. However, a few states have been able to report on these key attributes. Texas recently completed an exhaustive study of its felony sentencing patterns with special attention to the attributes of offenders sentenced to state prison.[8] That study reported the following sentencing patterns:

- 49 percent of convicted felons were sentenced to prison.
- 24 percent of the convicted felons sentenced to prison had no prior felony convictions.
- The most frequent crime resulting in a prison sentence was drug possession (22 percent) followed by burglary (20 percent), theft and fraud (20 percent), and drug delivery (15 percent). These four nonviolent crimes constitute 77 percent of all prison admissions.
- 53 percent of all drug offenders (possession and trafficking) sentenced to prison were convicted for possession of one gram or less of the illegal substance.

The Texas data, like that for many states, reflect the growing use of prison for incarcerating drug offenders. As shown in Table 2-1, one-fourth of all prison sentences in 1990 were for drug crimes, with half being for simple possession. In 1981, the proportion of prison admissions for drug crimes was only 9 percent; in 1960, the percentage was only 5 percent (Figure 2-3).[9] It is also no coincidence that as the proportion of prison admissions for drug crimes have increased, so have the proportions of nonwhites being sent to prison.

These quantitative studies suggest that a significant number of persons are being sentenced to prison for relatively minor crimes. This is not to say that there aren't offenders who are highly dangerous and need to be incarcerated for extensive periods of time. But what

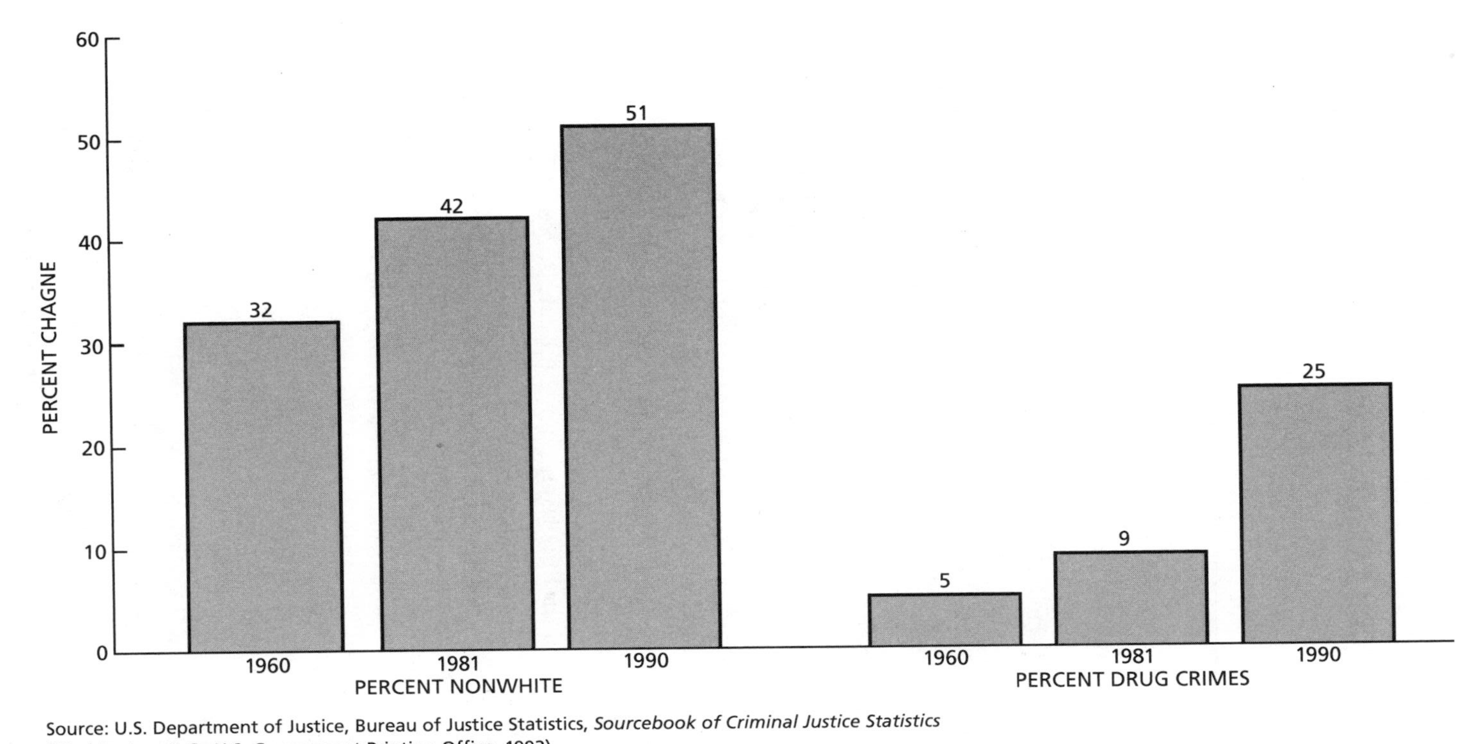

Source: U.S. Department of Justice, Bureau of Justice Statistics, *Sourcebook of Criminal Justice Statistics* (Washington, D.C.: U.S. Government Printing Office, 1992).

FIGURE 2-3 Percent Change in Proportions of Prison Admissions Who Are "Nonwhite" and for Drug Crimes, 1960, 1981, 1990

proportion of these half-million prisoners are truly dangerous and require long-term confinement? To answer this question, we undertook a more detailed analysis of today's prison population.

A CLOSER LOOK AT WHO GOES TO PRISON

Although the data cited earlier suggest a far less violent population serving lengthy periods of imprisonment, they are unable to paint a complete picture of the criminal lifestyles or the types of crimes committed by the present prison population. To fill in these blanks, we conducted an ethnographic study of 154 males sentenced to prison, randomly selected from the *intake* populations of three states (Washington, Nevada, and Illinois).[10]

We emphasize intake population because most studies of prison populations—such as the survey conducted every five years by the Bureau of Justice Statistics for the purpose of answering the question, in the agency director's words, "who goes to prison and why"—look at who is *in* prison at a particular point in time. This methodology provides a distorted picture of who is going to prison because those prisoners with longer sentences, usually sentenced for more serious crimes, stack up in the prison population and are overrepresented in one-day surveys.

The states we selected for our study varied in their sentencing structures, population sizes, rates of imprisonment, and lengths of imprisonment (Table 2-3). Illinois uses a determinate sentencing structure in which release occurs after a prisoner serves approximately 50 percent of the original sentence. Although a parole board exists, it has no authority to grant release. At the time of the study, Illinois had a large prison population (nearly 25,000 inmates) but a moderate rate of incarceration compared to other states (226 per 100,000 in 1989 versus the national average of 274 per 100,000). Although Illinois's determinate sentencing law eliminated discretionary release by the parole board, the vast majority of inmates must serve some period of parole supervision. Washington adopted sentencing guidelines with the specific goal of increasing lengths of stay for inmates convicted of violent crimes. It had a smaller prison population (approximately 7,000)

TABLE 2-3 Key Characteristics of Three State Prison Systems

Inmate Characteristic	Nevada	Illinois	Washington
I. Sentencing structure	indeterminate	determinate	guidelines
II. Inmate population (1989)	5,112	22,576	6,928
III. Annual admissions (1989)	3,052	14,567	4,155
A. New court commitments	2,514	10,732	3,543
B. Parole violators	509	3,693	401
C. Returned escapees	34	102	199
D. Other	0	40	12
IV. Incarceration rate (1989)	473	226	144
V. Releases (1989)			
Total	2,826	10,936	3,043
Parole/conditional	1,472	9,802	966
Unconditional	1,293	841	1,907
Other	61	293	170

Source: Nevada Department of Prisons, Illinois Department of Corrections, Washington Department of Corrections.

and a low incarceration rate (144 per 100,000). Because Washington eliminated parole as part of its sentencing guidelines reform act, very few inmates were released to parole or violators returned to prison. Nevada had a relatively smaller inmate population but the highest incarceration rate (473 per 100,000). It uses an indeterminate sentencing scheme that allows inmates to be released by a parole board after serving approximately 20 percent of the original sentence.

In selecting inmates to be interviewed for the study, we received lists of inmates admitted to reception centers during the prior two weeks. We then separated the names on these intake lists into the following five categories based on the most serious crime of conviction:

1. Violent crimes (murder, rape, assault, etc.)
2. Robbery (armed and unarmed)
3. Other theft (burglary, larceny, etc.)
4. Drug crimes (possession and trafficking)
5. All others

Our sample does not include women or persons readmitted to prison for parole violation who were convicted of no new felony. The exclusion of these two groups means that our sample is biased toward those persons who have committed the most serious crimes. In most cases, a parole violation is triggered by arrests for misdemeanor crimes or violations of supervision, such as failure to appear for office visits with parole agents or failure to attend a prescribed treatment program. Female prisoners tend to be convicted of less serious crimes.

For each state, we then randomly drew ten persons from each of the five categories, resulting in a total sample of 154.[11] We interviewed these persons in lengthy open interviews, covering their social histories, criminal activities in the period before the current arrest, and the full circumstances of their arrests. The information gathered from the interviews was verified and augmented by the arrest records along with police and probation office reports.

HOW SERIOUS ARE THEIR CRIMES?

An essential part of the public conception of street crime is that growing numbers of persons are engaged in very serious crime. To evaluate the severity of the crimes committed by inmates in our samples, we used an objective measure of seriousness from the public's perspective based on data gathered in 1980 by the Center for Studies in Criminology and Criminal Law at the University of Pennsylvania. In the center's survey of crime seriousness, a national survey asked 52,000 Americans to assign a numerical score to a short description of 204 criminal acts, which reflected the respondents' perceptions of the crimes' seriousness. For example, two of the acts described were "A person, using force steals property worth $10 from outside a building," and, "A person, using force, robs a victim of $1,000. No physical harm occurs." The center reduced these raw scores into "ratio scores," which indicated the relative severity of each crime.

We observed that if the acts involved minor injury, the threat of injury, theft over $1,000, the use of a weapon, use of heroin, or selling of marijuana, they received a score of more than 5 on the center's scale. We labeled these "medium serious" crimes. If they involved theft of over $10,000, serious injury, attempted murder, sales of heroin, smuggling narcotics, they received a score of more than 10. We considered these "serious" crimes. If they involved rape, manslaughter, homicide, a child victim, or kidnapping, they received a score of more than 15. We labeled these "very serious" crimes. Crimes that lack any of these characteristics received a score of less than 5. We called these petty crimes. Two such acts from the survey are: "A person breaks into a department store and steals merchandise worth $10" and "A person smokes marijuana."

We sorted the crimes of our sample into the categories "petty," "medium serious," "serious," and "very serious" according to these characteristics. Figure 2-4 summarizes the results of this distribution. In this figure we have adjusted our stratified samples so that they reflect the offense distribution for the nation as shown in Table 2-1.[12]

As Figure 2-4 reveals, most of the crimes for which persons are sent to prison (52.6 percent) fall into the petty categories. This finding is wholly consistent with inmate classification studies that have repeatedly found that most prisoners are committed to prison for petty offenses, with the result that the majority (50–70 percent) are classified as minimum-custody inmates.[13] The distribution on crime seriousness was somewhat different in the three states, as shown in Figure 2-5. Washington, which has the lowest rate of incarceration of the three states, also had the lowest proportion of petty felonies and the highest proportion of serious crimes. This is to be expected, as Washington

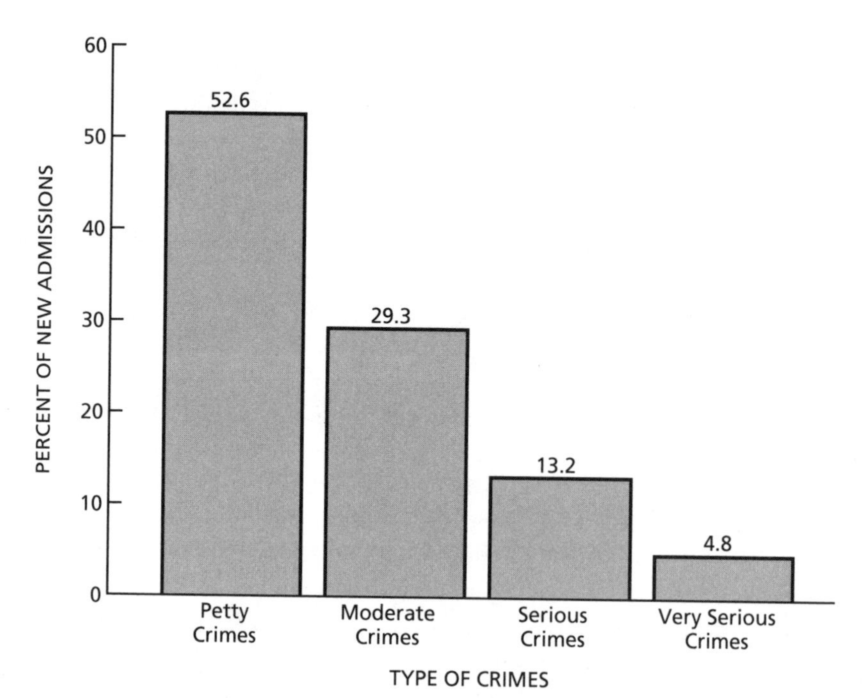

FIGURE 2-4 Severity of Crimes Committed by Persons Admitted to Prison National Estimate

recently enacted sentencing guidelines that purposely restrict the use of prison for nonviolent and property crimes.[14] Illinois, which has a medium rate, does not differ very much from the total sample. Nevada, which has the highest rate of the three states and the highest rate in the nation, predictably has the lowest proportion of serious and very serious crimes.

Our research indicates that over half the persons being sent to prison are being sent for petty crimes, which are crimes with no aggravating features—that is, no significant amount of money, no injury, or any other feature that would cause ordinary citizens to view the crime as particularly serious. The following are narrative descriptions of three typical petty crimes from our sample:

> George, a 17-year-old black youth, was arrested for possession of a stolen vehicle. He had been kicked out of school in the

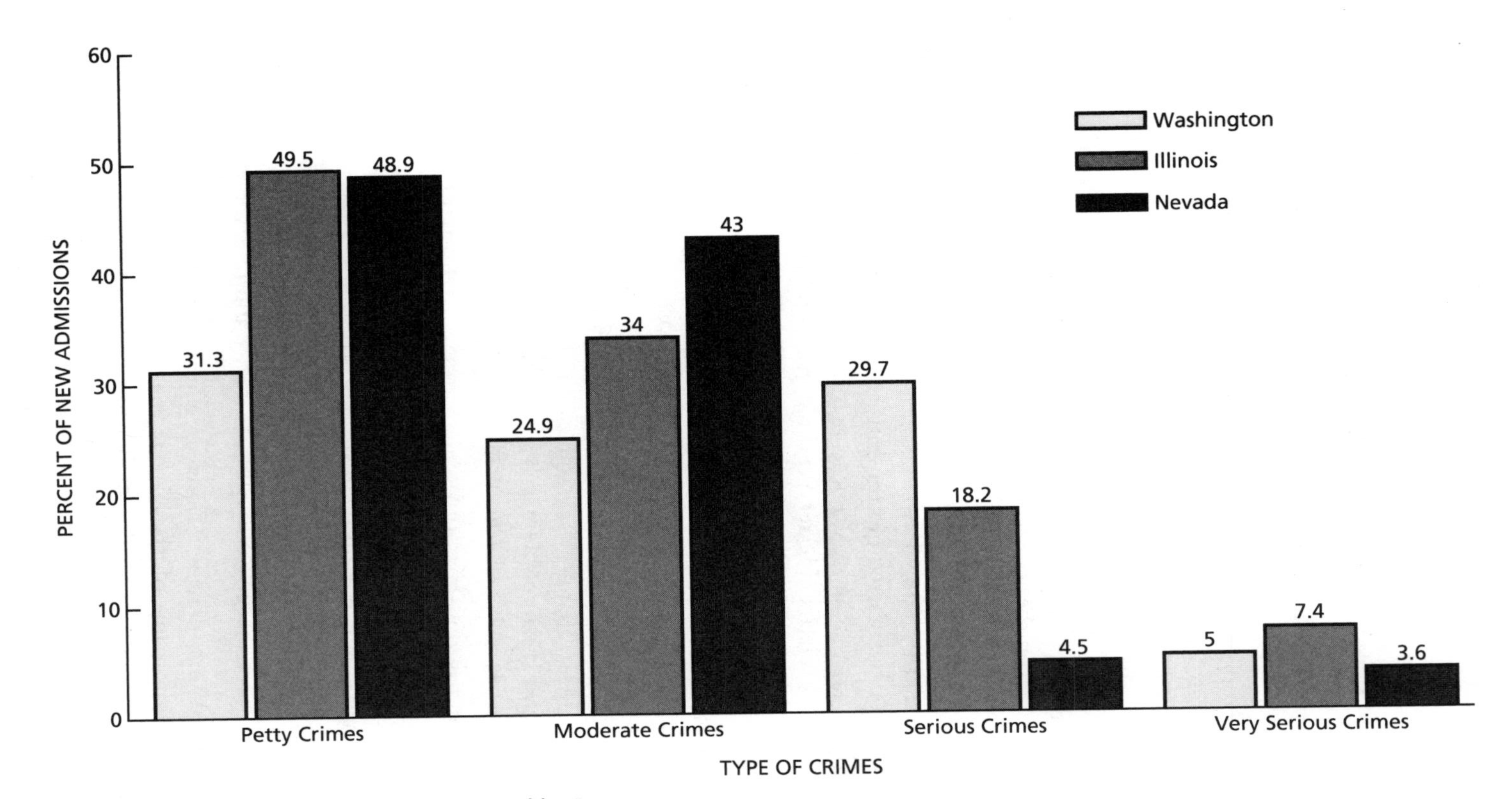

FIGURE 2-5 Severity of Crimes Committed by Persons Admitted to Prison, Washington, Illinois, and Nevada

ninth grade. Since then, he had worked at a couple of jobs—a small soul food restaurant and a small garage fixing cars. He hadn't been working for a while. He had been arrested a few times before—once for curfew, another for shoplifting. A couple of months before this arrest, he was arrested for "busting a car window." "A man tried to hit me with his car and I swung at him and broke his window. I got three months supervision." On the current arrest he was caught inside a car tying to steal the radio. "They said I busted the window, but it weren't locked. He [the policeman] took the screwdriver I was using and put it in the lock and said I was stealing the car." He was sentenced to three years.

Jimmy, a 26-year-old black man, dropped out of high school in the tenth grade. He worked at several unskilled jobs as a teenager but started getting into trouble when he was 17. After several arrests, he was sent to prison for aggravated assault against a relative. He served three years and then another year and a half for violation of parole. He had been out for two months when he was arrested this time. He was living with his grandmother, "trying to stay out of trouble." He was not able to find a job and was living on general assistance. He was caught in an abandoned school where he and some other young men were looking for junk metal which they intended to sell for "some loose change." The school had been abandoned for six years and local people had been stealing from it repeatedly. He received seven years for burglary.

Edmond is a 50-year-old white carpenter who works in Florida in the winter and Seattle in the summer. He had been arrested once 22 years ago for receiving stolen property. He was passing through Las Vegas on his way to Seattle and says he found a billfold with $100 on a bar where he was drinking and gambling. The owner, who suspected him of taking it, turned him in. He was charged with grand larceny and received three years.

Twenty-nine percent of our sample fell into the medium serious category, but many of these were aggravated because the charges involved possession or sales of heroin or cocaine. Acts in the 1980 national public opinion survey with heroin involved had a score of seven or more. We assumed that cocaine, which was not mentioned in the survey, would be given approximately the same value today. However, most of our sample's heroin or cocaine crimes involved only very small amounts of the drugs and the persons, if they were dealers, were small fry, as the following cases indicate.

> Luis, a 29-year-old Puerto Rican raised in Chicago, had never been arrested before. He had been a member of Latin gangs but in recent years had less and less contact with them. He used cocaine occasionally and hung around with a lot of guys who dealt cocaine. He was riding with a friend on a motorcycle and the police pulled them over because they were not wearing helmets. The police found a packet of cocaine on his friend and several on the ground around them. He and his friend were charged with possession of cocaine. Luis was sentenced to three years.
>
> Felix had been in trouble on the west side of Chicago since he was 10 years old. He dropped out of school in the eighth grade and was arrested several times before he was 18. He served three prison terms since then. Now, at 26, he was living at home with his mother, "taking little side jobs," and hustling a little. He says he wants "an average job and to go home after it and enjoy life." On the present arrest, he was riding with his girlfriend and the police stopped them. They said they had a report that a man and a woman were selling drugs out of a car in that neighborhood. They found one bag of cocaine (.5 grams) on his girlfriend's side of the car and arrested him. He was sentenced to two years.

Robberies were considered at least medium serious because the public, officials, and criminologists invariably view robbery as a serious crime and a violent crime (government agencies that compile statistics on crimes always place robbery in their "violent" category). In actuality, however, many robberies differ from the public's perception of them. The following, for example, do not seem to fit the image, and many citizens, perhaps a majority, would not consider them serious or violent crimes:

> Darryl was a 21-year-old black man raised on the south side of Chicago in housing projects. He dropped out of school in the tenth grade and had been working on and off at minimum-wage jobs. He had been arrested three times for minor crimes (battery,

disorderly conduct, and marijuana) and had no convictions. In this case, he had gone to a neighborhood drug dealer to borrow some money on his girlfriend's watch because his "brother was coming to town and I wanted to have some money to do things with him." The dealer offered him $60, but only gave him $20, telling him that he would give him $40 later. Darryl did not see the dealer for two weeks and when he finally encountered him and asked him for the money, the dealer said he didn't have any and offered Darryl drugs. When he was showing him the drugs, Darryl saw the watch and he grabbed for it. They fought and the drug dealer was "whipping" him. Darryl's brother jumped in and helped him. Then the dealer gave Darryl the watch. Three days later, the police came to his apartment and arrested him for robbery and assault. He was bailed out and later went to a jury trial. The jury found him not guilty on aggravated assault and was hung on the robbery. However, Darryl had run from the court while they were deliberating. He later turned himself in, bail was set at $150,000, and the public defender talked him into pleading guilty to robbery. He was sentenced to prison for three years.

Richard graduated from high school in Seattle and went into the armed services. After being discharged, he went to cosmetology school and worked for thirteen years as a cosmetologist. Three years ago he began learning a new trade and worked part time in a print shop. He had started using marijuana and heroin in high school. When he was working as a cosmetologist, he and his wife "got into coke, heavy." He had several arrests for driving while under the influence and one for child molesting. "That was a mistake. I was drunk and high and I just got carried away with this young girl." After this last arrest, he and his wife decided to change their lives and quit all drugs. "I became responsible and became manager of Super Cuts. But after a while, I got bored and started hanging around with my old friends. They were freebasing and pretty soon I was back into drugs heavy. I left my wife and moved in with a friend. I couldn't believe that I had let my life get so fucked up again, so I went into a drug program, but I didn't get along with the director. After three weeks I tried coke again. And I was right back into

> the same lifestyle. I needed money, so I decided to rob some stores. I robbed the same store three times, a convenience store like 7-Eleven. I got about $50 each time. I tucked a BB gun in my belt and went in, showed the clerk the gun in my belt, and asked for the money. In court the clerk said I was polite." He was sentenced to five years.

There were many serious and some very serious crimes in our samples. Two were very serious armed robberies (they involved larger amounts of money and persons were threatened during the robberies). There were seven first-degree homicides (2.2 percent of our adjusted samples), and three were gang related. The following is one:

> Parnell, a 20-year-old member of the Disciples, had dropped out of school and hung around with his neighborhood branch of the gang since he was 15. He had never held a job and was arrested 14 or 15 times for activities related to "gang banging,"[15] mostly possession of weapons. He was arrested once for robbery when he was 17. "The guy I was walking with strong-armed some guy. But I wasn't into robbing, just gang banging." The night of the murder, he and some of his gang were at a skating rink, which was the location of many hostilities between rival gangs. His group saw a guy from another gang who they thought had robbed one of their buddies. They chased him and one of them beat him with a baseball bat. He died a week later. P. was the only one convicted because "I was the only one a witness identified." He received 25 years.

Two occurred during drug robberies. This is one of them:

> Anthony, a 24-year-old black man, was sent to prison when he was 17 for aggravated battery. "Some guy broke out the windows of a neighbor of mine. I went to court and after the court a fight broke out and they arrested all of us." After serving 18 months, he completed two years in community college and had been working for five years as a roofer. He says he was living a clean life in the suburbs of Chicago, working, playing basketball, taking care of his common-law wife and her son. "They said I went to this house, kicked in the door and demanded drugs and money, and then shot the man. The woman in the house identified me. The police had received an anonymous

> phone call and they arrested me. They said I searched the house, but they didn't find any fingerprints. The description she gave the police didn't fit me."

In two cases, persons were convicted of killing their girlfriends. In one, a 33-year-old Cuban man who had never been in trouble before and who had worked steadily, was convicted of killing his girlfriend:

> It was an accident. I was fighting with my girlfriend. She bothered me a lot. I had a son with her and she was wanted me to leave my wife. We had been drinking and we got into a fight. I hit her with my fist and killed her.

Most of the serious crimes (53 percent) were sex crimes. These ranged from child molesting to rape, and most were acts committed against family members or close associates. These are serious crimes, but it should be noted again that most of them depart from the popular images of crime and criminals in which a menacing stranger is the perpetrator. The other serious crimes were robberies (17 percent), attempted murders (8 percent), manslaughters (12 percent), and drug charges (10 percent). Several of the robberies and drug crimes *do* approach the popular image: that is, they involved larger amounts of money, threats or injuries to victims, or larger amounts of cocaine or heroin.

PATTERNS OF CRIME

As we suggested earlier, the public and many officials believe that most street criminals are "career criminals" or "high-rate offenders" who, if free, will commit many felonies. Some public officials and criminologists have recommended that these high-rate offenders be "incapacitated" through long prison terms:

> Today, the concept of the career is entrenched in criminal justice—a dramatic rethinking of policy and practice. Now research is examining ways to identify those offenders more accurately, moving toward the recommendation of one recent study that concluded that public safety would clearly benefit from incarcerating a larger proportion of high-risk probationers and prisoners, and for longer periods of time.[16]

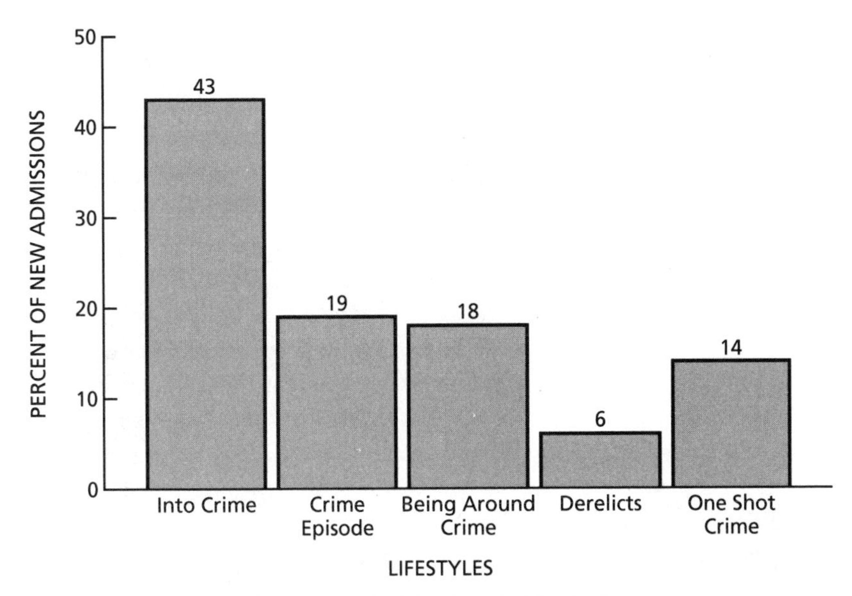

FIGURE 2-6 Criminal Lifestyles for Newly Admitted Prisoners

Though no specific program to do this has been introduced in the United States, legislators, judges, and prosecutors have passed laws to extend sentences, have recommended longer sentences, or have granted longer sentences because they hold this belief in the prevalence of high-rate offenders.

To test the validity of the "career criminal" viewpoint, we focused on patterns of offending among our surveyed convicts. We discovered five distinct patterns—"into crime," "crime episode," "one-shot crime," "being around crime," and "dereliction," which are defined and summarized below. Figure 2-6 indicates the proportion of our sample that corresponds to each crime pattern.

Into Crime (43 percent). Persons into crime call themselves thieves, "hustlers," "dope fiends," or "gang bangers," which they understand as identities within particular criminal systems. They also follow the patterns of crime consistent with these identities and criminal systems—that is, they attempt to steal large amounts of money through burglaries and robberies; they "hustle" on the streets, making money any way they can; they maintain drug habits by selling drugs and stealing;

or they hang out with their fellow "homeboys," wear their gang's colors, steal, and fight with other gangs. Parnell, described earlier, was a gang banger into crime. Bertram, a thief, and Donald, a dope fiend, were into crime:

> Bertram says he "started a life of crime" when he was in high school. When he was 17, every weekday, he and older friends walked from their neighborhood on the south side of Chicago to Hyde Park, a middle-class white neighborhood, and burglarized some houses. They took TVs, jewelry, and any other thing they could sell. "It was like a job." They were caught in one house and arrested. Bertram was sentenced to three years in prison. When he got out of prison, his brother and sisters were living alone and his younger brother was selling cocaine. Bertram stopped him, but he had to supply them with money. So he started burglarizing houses and trucks on the west side at night. Then he and his "rappies" pulled 16 armed robberies of gas stations and convenience stores. In one week, he says, they made $7,000 apiece. After the last robbery, they were pulled over by the police, who found guns in their car. He received 10 years.

> Donald started using heroin and cocaine when he was 19. He was convicted of burglary when he was 25 and served six months in the county jail. He was convicted of possession of drugs when he was 29 and received a year in the state prison. As soon as he got out, he was arrested again for burglary and served four years. He says he did not want to go back to drugs, but he met a friend right after getting out and got high with him. He was quickly addicted and stealing again. He says he was pulling one or two burglaries a day. He could not sell drugs because the police knew him too well. In his last arrest, he was caught trying to pry open a door of a construction business and was convicted of two attempted burglaries. At 33, he says he wants to stop using drugs, but he doesn't know how. He says he is getting tired.

Since they were committing crime regularly, it is accurate to view the 43 percent of our sample who were "into crime" as high-rate offenders. Of these high-rate offenders, more than half (57 percent) had served a prior prison sentence and 32 percent a juvenile sentence.

However, most of the active offenders (59 percent) were convicted of petty crimes. All of our data strongly suggest that, rather than being vicious predators, most were disorganized, unskilled, undisciplined petty criminals who very seldom engaged in violence or made any significant amount of money from their criminal acts.

Crime Episode (19 percent). These inmates had engaged in a crime episode or spree. Many had committed crimes in some earlier period; some had even been "into crime." Unlike the into-crime group, these offenders had less severe histories of prior incarcerations, either as adults (33 percent had a prior prison term) or as juveniles (26 percent had a prior juvenile record). But for an extended period, perhaps after a jail or prison sentence, they had lived a relatively conventional life:

> Joe joined a Latin gang when he was 13. By his eighteenth year he had been arrested three times in activities with his "home-boys" (the Latin Kings). For the last, a residential burglary, he served a county jail sentence and was placed on probation for two years. After that, he pulled back from gang banging but was still hanging around with some of his old friends. "We hung around the corner drinking, but we didn't think of ourselves as a gang. We thought of ourselves as an organization. We tried to protect all the old people, to stop the blacks from robbing them." He was working steadily at the Golden Grain packing house making $7 an hour. "I was going to work there the rest of my life." He had a car and a girlfriend and they were buying furniture—a bedroom set. The crime he was convicted of occurred early on a Sunday morning. He had been partying at a house with his friend —"smoking, drinking, and snorting." Someone borrowed his car and didn't bring it back to the house. He was angry about this. A friend gave him a ride home and on the way, he said, "Someone said: 'Let's go rob someone.' I guess I said, 'Let's go, I'll do it.' I don't remember much about it. A white guy was stabbed in the stomach and neck. For all I know, the other guy in the car did it. It was stupid. I blacked out from the time I got home until the police came." He received six years for attempted murder.
>
> Richard was one of the few black students in his high school in Montana and the star football player. He was also selling drugs.

"I scored five touchdowns on Friday and was busted on Monday. I was hanging around white kids trying to prove myself. They wouldn't let me play football after that." His father put him out of the house, so he left for Oklahoma with some friends. He returned to Montana but couldn't find a job. He began hanging around some of the black guys who were "going to discos and being cool." He was arrested for a house burglary and received two years' probation. He went to California with a friend who was in the Air Force. He joined the army, got married and had two kids. He had broke up with his wife by the time he was discharged from the army. He stayed in Fort Lewis, Washington and worked part time in construction, living across the street from a corner where drugs were being sold. "One night I walked over there and a guy asked me if I wanted to make some money. So I started selling drugs. I sold to the police. They wanted me to set up my supplier, so I went back to the corner, but the word had got out, so the other dealers told me to get out of town." He went back to California and went back to his wife. They both used cocaine heavily. He turned himself into a drug program, but she continued to use cocaine. He went back to the house and found her in bed with another man. He kicked the man out and took his son. He was charged with kidnapping his child and served two years in a California prison. He was transferred to Washington upon release and charged with unlawful delivery of drugs for the earlier arrest. He received 15 months.

Being Around Crime (18 percent). About one-fifth of our sample were "corner boys," men who were raised and lived in lower-class neighborhoods in which street crime is a prominent feature. Many in these neighborhoods, particularly young males, regularly commit crimes. Most other young males avoid regular participation in crime but accept it as a normal feature of life around them. Many of the males, particularly younger males, though they avoid regular involvement in crime and do not think of themselves as criminals, are at risk of being arrested because they are on the streets for many hours and police regularly patrol these neighborhoods looking for street criminals. When confronted by police, these corner boys or lower-class men also frequently exhibit macho behavior that provokes hostile reactions from the police. Finally, corner boys are often present at crimes being committed by friends or relatives, and, under special circumstances—such as when they are in the company of more criminally oriented acquaintances, saving face in front of peers, intoxicated, or trying to take advantage of an opportunity for a financial gain—they are drawn into the commission of a crime.

Once arrested, their corner boy or lower-class identity makes it very likely that police, district attorneys, and judges will treat these young men as if they were more criminally involved than they actually were. Sixty-eight percent of our corner boys were convicted of petty crimes. Only a small minority had adult prior terms (8 percent) and/or juvenile terms (15 percent). The cases of Darryl and Robert described in the section on crime seriousness are examples of this pattern. The following are two more.

> Maurice is an 18-year-old black youth raised on the south side of Chicago. He was in the Disciples from ages 12 to 16, but he dropped out. "My grandmother told me to get out of the gang. They hate it when you pull out, so they were right at my door waiting for me." He dropped out of high school in the tenth grade. He had gotten into a little trouble before—some fights and the theft of a Moped, for which he received two years' probation. "A guy let me ride it. I didn't know he had stole it." At the time of this arrest, he was staying off the streets. "I had a girlfriend with two kids. She lived with her father. I would go over to her house and stay all day. We'd sit around and watch TV, clean the house, help with the kids." On the day of this arrest, he was going to his grandmother's to get something and a policeman who worked in that area stopped him to question him. "There's a guy around there that looks like me. He would get into a few things. The police asked what was I doing over there. I wrestled with him and his gun fell out of his holster. I kicked it and ran. They got me later. They found out I didn't do nothing so they charged me with taking his gun." He received five years for disarming a police officer.

> Eddie is a 32-year-old black man raised in Little Rock, Arkansas. His mother supported the family of six kids. She worked as a cook in a motel and they lived in a housing project. He quit school in the ninth grade and went to work as a busboy

in the motel. He worked there for seven years, ending up as a cook. He got married in Little Rock to a woman with a daughter. They moved to Seattle, where he worked at several jobs, the last one as a supervisor of a janitorial crew in a federal building. Years before, the police had arrested him in an apartment he managed. The charge was dismissed. This was his only prior arrest. In Seattle he spent a lot of time playing basketball. He was on a team sponsored by the Mormons. He was the top player and scored 36 points one game. He started hanging around one of the other players who was using a lot of cocaine. Eddie says he "sort of took this guy under his wing." He started using cocaine with him. His wife objected to this, so Eddie stopped. He says he was trying to get his friend to stop also. One night he took his friend to his friend's apartment to collect some money from his roommate. Eddie stayed in the car. The friend and the roommate got into a fight over the money, and the friend ended up stabbing the roommate. The roommate accused both of them of robbing him and Eddie was arrested for robbery. He was released on his own recognizance, but after a week the supervisor said she did not want to supervise him. He was held in the county jail for five months and finally he pleaded guilty. The public defender told him since he had admitted being there he would not be able to win a trial. "I decided I was going ahead and get it over with and get on with my life." He received five years for robbery.

Dereliction (4 percent). These men had completely lost the capacity to live in organized society. Some had teetered on the edge of physical survival. All had been incarcerated a lot in early life, and most used drugs and alcohol, usually from their early teens. Though they tried to avoid committing serious crimes (to avoid returning to prison), they occasionally robbed, burgled, or committed some other felony (e.g., arson, assault, sexual deviations) and were arrested. Though their crimes were invariably very petty, their repulsive disreputability and their former records resulted in imprisonment. This group had the highest prior prison record (91 percent), with 71 percent incarcerated as juveniles.[17] The following are two examples of their crimes and lifestyles:

Leonard is a 32-year-old black man who grew up on the south side of Chicago. His father died when he was small and his mother raised seven children on welfare. He dropped out of school in the ninth grade and never had a steady job. He was a Disciple until his early 20s. He started to drink heavily when he was a teenager. He was first arrested when he was 15 and again when he was 17. Both times he was sent to youth institutions. He was arrested for robbery and auto theft as an adult and served two prison terms. He lived with his mother and says all he does is drink. Three years ago it was discovered that he had cirrhosis of the liver. Two years before this imprisonment, he and a friend robbed another black man on the street. This man lived in the neighborhood and knew them. His friend had a stick and they were charged with robbery. Leonard received probation, but he quit reporting and they arrested him and sentenced him to five years.

Charles and his three sisters were raised by his nurse mother on the south side of Chicago. He "got to drinking and smoking reefer at about ten." He was hanging around with the "bad kids" and not going to school. He started getting into trouble with the police and then "they started harassing me." He was in a small local gang and they got into a lot of fights. Later he joined the "Gangster Disciples," a splinter of the Disciples. He has never held a steady job. He was arrested when he was 16 for not going to school and was sent to a boys' school. He ran away and was sent to another youth institution. When he was 17, he was arrested for robbery and was sent to Stateville [Illinois State Prison] for six months. When he was 22, he was convicted of another robbery and sent back to prison for five years. For the last five years, he has been a derelict. He stays high or drunk most of the time. "I been stealing petty things, anything you can take from a store. I quit robbery. Made a believer out of me. I been 'carrying a stick' [no residence and sleeping anywhere he could]." Some days before this arrest, he went to the house of a girlfriend and a man came to the door. "I asked him for my girlfriend and he said 'Fuck you, punk.' I went to his car and hit it with a water-meter cover I picked up off the street. He came after me with a hatchet and hit me in the head. I went to the hospital and when I got out I went over and smashed his car. Then a week later, I started a fire in a old building next to his house. My old girlfriend told them who did it. I was drunk at the time." He received four years for attempted arson.

One-Shot Crime (14 percent). A significant number of our sample had never been involved in serious crime before the current arrest. Something about the crime—its seriousness or an associated mandatory sentence—resulted in their receiving a prison sentence. The following are two of these crimes.

> José was born in Puerto Rico and his father sent for him to come to Massachusetts when José was 10. He quit high school when he was a junior. He joined the army when he was 20 "to get a G.E.D." and was discharged three years later. He worked as a baker for the next 10 years for Nabisco. He quit this job to help a friend run a grocery store. Then he worked for five years with Sanco, until the firm moved to Philadelphia in 1983, four years ago. He hasn't found a steady job since. He has been married for 20 years and has four daughters. At 46 he had no steady job and was drinking a lot. He had a friend who deals in cocaine. A narcotics undercover officer who had been trying to set up his friend repeatedly asked José to buy some cocaine for him. He finally did and was arrested. He was out on bail for two and a half years before sentencing, but the sentence was mandatory.
>
> Donald was raised on a farm in Iowa. Two years after graduating from high school, he went into business for himself, leasing livestock. At 30, he changed businesses and has been selling mobile home running gear ever since. He was married for 10 years, but separated five years ago. He has been arrested for failure to pay child support, but nothing else. He was drinking heavily in the last year of his marriage, but has just about quit drinking. Now all he does is "work my ass off in my business. I have been working seven days a week. Most of the time I am on the road with two helpers, delivering mobile home running gear." Three years ago, he and two employees were making a delivery with a large truck and trailer. After dinner, they picked up a six-pack and a little later they stopped on the side of the

road in a rural area of Illinois to urinate. He and one of the employees got back into the cab of the truck. He says he thought the other employee, a 16-year old (who had told Donald he was 18) was also in the cab, but he wasn't and he was run over by the truck when Donald pulled out onto the highway. "He might have been trying to get on the trailer and fell under the wheels." They accused him of being drunk, although he says he only had a couple of beers. "They never ran a test on me and the officer who arrested me testified that I didn't have alcohol on my breath." Donald was convicted of reckless homicide and sent to prison for a year.

HABITUAL OFFENDERS

Even though most offenders are sent to prison for less than serious felonies and for short sentences (e.g. 24 months), a growing number receive very long sentences, many life. This is mainly because many states and the federal government have passed laws that mandate that certain offenders be sentenced to prison under "habitual offender" or "mandatory" sentence laws, which require inmates to spend a minimum of 10 years or longer, or to be sentenced to life without the possibility of parole (i.e., they must die in prison).

According to the Criminal Justice Institute, as of January 1992, there were 13,937 inmates serving "natural" life sentences, 52,054 serving life with the possibility of parole, and 125,996 serving sentences of 20 years or longer.[18] In other words, nearly 200,000 of the 862,761 state and federal prisoners were serving extremely long sentences. An unknown but probably high percent of these were serving time under these restrictive laws. One would expect that these laws are reserved for only the most vicious and dangerous offenders, but recent studies suggest otherwise.

One study completed by the Correction Association of New York reported on the types of inmates who were serving mandatory prison sentences for drug offenses, repeat felony convictions, and violent crimes.[19] In the 1970s, the New York Legislature passed a number of laws that mandated a prison term for persons convicted of certain drug crimes, violent offenses (robbery, assault, murder, manslaughter, rape) or persons who had prior felony convictions. At the time of this study nearly two thirds of all prisoners were sentenced under one of these three laws (8 percent drug, 14.5 percent repeat felony, and 41.5 percent violent offender laws).

The research consisted of selecting a small (21) but representative sample of inmates who were sentenced via these mandatory sentencing laws and developing detailed case histories of the crimes they had committed but also their life circumstances. In its report, the researchers concluded that many of these inmates, while "not boy scouts" do not deserve the type of sentences they have received. What follows are two examples:

- BERNICE LANE—Mandatory Drug Sentence—15 Years to Life—Criminal Sale of Controlled Substance in the First Degree

  In November 1977, Bernice Lane was found guilty after trial of criminal sale of a controlled substance in the first degree and conspiracy in the first degree. According to the district attorney's office, Lane, a hotel manager who lived with her mother, had sold a total of 2.9 ounces of heroin to undercover officers in Manhattan in two separate transactions in 1976.

  It was Lane's first conviction, but not her first arrest. In 1966, drug possession charges were filed against her but were later dropped when authorities arranged a guilty plea with her co-defendant, a known drug dealer. Eight years later, conspiracy charges were filed but also dropped after authorities failed to produce an informant who, they said, could have linked Lane to a major drug ring.

  The judge at Lane's trial, former Supreme (now Appellate) Court Judge Ernst H. Rosenberger, said that had the law not prevented him, he would have ordered a more lenient sentence than 15 years to life, the minimum required in Lane's case. ". . . I do not feel that the acts of the defendant . . . warrant a life imprisonment," Rosenberger stated. Lane was also sentenced to zero to seven years for conspiracy; the sentences were to run concurrently.

  Lane was 46 when she entered Bedford Hills Correctional Facility. She lived on the honor floor and took part in both the Long Termers and the Pre-Release Committees. She helped design a Career Awareness Program to prepare inmates for work after release. One professional associated with the prison called Lane "a mature and capable woman who is held in high regard by both peers and staff."

Almost four and half years later, Judge Rosenberger ruled on a motion from Lane's new attorney that Lane had been the victim of ineffective counsel. The judge vacated Lane's conviction and dismissed the indictment.

Freed without supervision on February 12, 1982, Lane returned home to care for her aging mother. She soon found work as a rental assistant with a property management company in the South Bronx. There, according to one of her supervisors, she was granted two pay raises and given the responsibility of opening the office with her own set of keys. "She gave more time than necessary," said Dialis Romero, manager of Two Trees Management Inc. Another supervisor said that Lane showed "concern and compassion" in her work.

Lane also did volunteer work. According to Rosemary O'Regan, executive director of Tender Loving Crafts, a business that sells inmate crafts, Lane worked "tirelessly and enthusiastically" in her spare time for the nonprofit company. Lane also sat on the board of directors of the nursing home where she helped serve lunch every day. "[Bernice Lane] is loved and adored here," reported Doris Terry, founder of the center. "She is an asset to the community."

But on April 12, 1983, the Appellate Division unanimously reversed Rosenberger's decision. The court ruled that Lane had not been denied effective assistance of counsel, reinstated the original conviction, and ordered her to return to prison.

Supporters were stunned. "She lived at home with her mother, she had a good job and she was a taxpayer," stated Doris Terry. "She was rehabilitated. Isn't that what the criminal justice system is all about?" On November 14, 1983, after all appeals failed, Lane traveled to Bedford Hills unescorted and turned herself in.

Today Bernice Lane, 54, still takes part in the Long Termers Committee and the Career Awareness Program. She is also taking courses in data processing. Her prison counselor calls her "an excellent human being . . . who just doesn't belong here." Bernice Lane's mother now lives by herself. Friends say she is growing frail. She is visited once a week by a staff member from the center where Lane did volunteer work.

Lane was denied clemency in 1984. She will be eligible for parole release when she is almost 65.

■ HENRY BARKER — Mandatory Violent Felony Law—15 Years to Life—Felony Murder

When two New York City Department of Correction bounty hunters arrested Henry Barker in 1978, they believed they had captured a dangerous criminal. A convicted murderer, Barker had escaped to Miami, where he lived undetected for almost three years. By the time they returned to New York, the bounty hunters, Steven Levy and Marvin Badler, had become Barker's supporters. "Under unbelievable circumstances, Henry Barker has straightened himself out, rehabilitated himself and has become a benefit to society," Badler told *The New York Times*.

Raised in the Bay Ridge section of Brooklyn, Barker graduated from Fort Hamilton High School and found a job as a runner on Wall Street. He drifted into handyman work, and in 1974 ended up painting tenements for a landlord, Samuel Richards. Richards later laid Barker off and, Barker claimed, withheld $200 owed him in back wages.

Barker made plans to retrieve the money by theft. He stood watch on the street while, inside Richard's apartment building, a friend attempted to steal the 76-year-old man's wallet. Richards was fatally stabbed in a scuffle. Barker tried to save him, placing a pillow under his head, putting an ice pack on his chest, and calling an ambulance. Cooperating with police, Barker was arrested a few days later and was subsequently indicted on charges of intentional murder and felony murder.[20] Barker had only one previous conviction: carrying a concealed weapon (a knife), for which he served three months' probation.

Barker claimed the violence was never intended, and that he did not know about his friend's knife. The presentence report stated that Barker was a "... sincere, somewhat misguided youth who did not impress this writer as a dangerous individual." Nevertheless, his court-appointed lawyer persuaded Barker to plead guilty to felony murder and accept the mandatory mini-

> mum sentence of 15 years to life—a better fate, the lawyer argued, than going to trial and facing a possible maximum of 25 to life. Two months after being sentenced, Barker fled Riker's Island.
>
> In Miami, he built a life for himself, often working three jobs at once. Using the name Tommy Prendergast, he won the affection of merchants, neighbors and employers—many of whom called him "Our Tommy" in letters now in Barker's file. "In a very short time, we and most other[s] . . . were treating him as if he was our son," reported one woman for whom Barker had worked. A man for whom Barker had provided housing and found a job wrote, "There should be a world full of human beings like him." At the time of this capture, he was working full time as a motel maintenance man and supporting his female companion and her three teenage daughters.
>
> Employed as a hospital dietitian at Green Haven Correctional Facility, Barker, now 35, is performing work that supervisors say is "over and above" the basic requirements. In August 1984 he graduated with a degree in psychology from Marist College with a B-plus average. Seven officers from the honor block at Great Meadow Correctional Facility, his first assignment, wrote letters of support for his unsuccessful commutation application. One called him a "respectable guy . . . a sincere person who cares about the people around him . . ."
>
> The judge in Barker's case, Leonard Scholnick, has written: "After careful consideration, it is my opinion that neither he [Barker] nor society would benefit from any further incarceration." Under mandatory sentencing statutes, however, Barker must serve the full 15-year minimum before being considered for parole.

A second and more recent study was conducted by NCCD to evaluate the effects of Florida's habitual sentencing laws.[21] In Florida, there are two situations that may trigger the court's decision to apply the Habitual Offender statute. The most common occurs for offenders who have two or more prior felony convictions. However, there is another provision called the Violent Habitual statute that permits an offender who has a prior felony conviction for a violent offense to be "habitualized." Habituals will serve approximately 10 years before they will be released with no parole supervision. By 1997, they will represent one fourth of the entire prison population.

The decision to apply the statute rests with the State Attorney. As it turns out, only about one fifth of all cases that meet the criteria for habitualization actually have them applied. The NCCD study found that this high degree of discretion results in significant racial bias in the application of the law. An analysis comparing the attributes of offenders who were habitualized versus those who were not found that black inmates were nearly twice as likely to receive an habitual sentence even when controlling for the offender's offense and prior criminal record.

A sample of 90 male and female inmates sentenced under the Habitual Offender sentencing laws in September and November, 1992, were drawn at random at four prison facilities and interviewed. They were characterized in the following manner:

- They tend to be not married (74 percent), with at least one child (69 percent), employed full (54 percent) or part-time (13 percent) but in a low paying occupation;
- A significant number (43 percent) have not completed their high school diploma, with very few advancing to college (8 percent);
- A small but sizeable number reported having histories of sexual abuse as a child or as an adult (27 percent), and/or histories of mental illness (16 percent).
- The vast majority were convicted of either a property crime (44 percent) or a drug crime (24 percent);
- Within the drug category virtually all of the crimes were related to crack cocaine;
- Nearly two-thirds were using drugs at the time the crime was committed (64 percent);
- In one-fifth of the crimes (usually drug crimes) there were no victims. The majority of the crimes where a victim was identified were inflicted upon strangers, businesses or law enforcement personnel (resisting arrest, assault, etc.);
- In 87 percent of the crimes there was no injury to the victim;
- In those instances where a property loss was suffered by the victim, the median loss was $300.

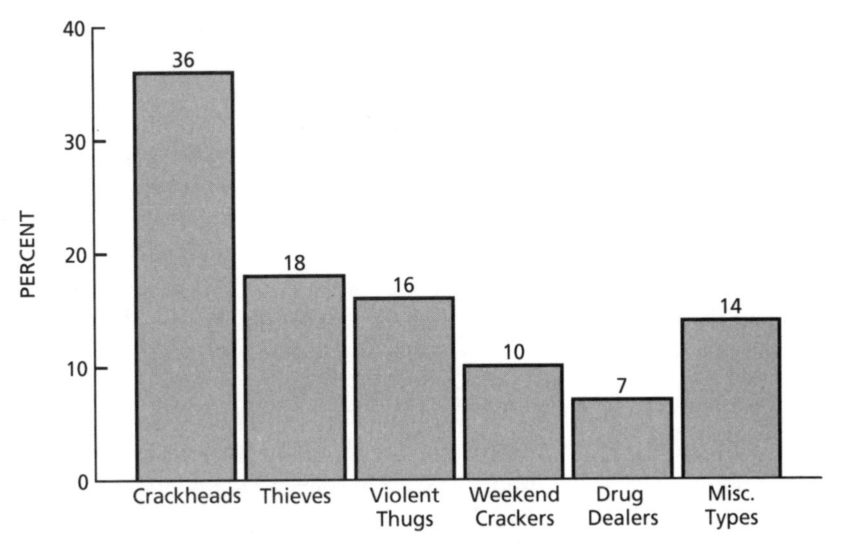

FIGURE 2-7 Proportion of Criminal Lifestyles of Interviewed Inmates Sentenced as Habitual Offenders

Using these data, each inmate was classified according to a criminal career typology reflecting their criminal lifestyle, including both the official data contained in the inmate's file and data from our interviews. The basic categories that were developed are discussed below as well as the proportion of cases that fell into these categories (Figure 2-7):

1. Crack-heads (36 percent)

   These offenders were characterized by their severe addiction to crack cocaine. Daily use of crack is part of their lifestyle. They would do virtually anything to maintain their drug habits. Typically they were not employed, hung around other crack-heads, and engaged in a wide variety of petty property crimes or petty drug trafficking to support their drug habits. They probably represent the most difficult drug cases to treat.

2. Weekend Crack Bingers (10 percent)

   Unlike the Crack-heads, these individuals used crack cocaine for recreational purposes—typically in the context of a weekend binge. They frequently were fully employed in blue-collar jobs and maintained relatively stable and normal outside interests. Because of their employability, they were frequently arrested through sting operations.

3. Regular Thieves (18 percent)

   There were two types of thieves. Those who were alcoholics, who, when under the influence of the drug, would attempt inept property crimes. They are incapable of holding a regular job or sustaining a marriage. The other typology reflected skillful thieves who typify the predatory offender. These offenders are rarely involved in other forms of illicit drug-use.

4. Violent Thugs (16 percent)

   This group reflected the most dangerous group of offenders to public safety. They frequently are involved in violent activities as part of their criminal lifestyles and rely upon violence and the use of weapons to commit their crimes.

5. Drug Dealers (7 percent)

   This group consists of inmates who do not abuse drugs but make a living selling drugs for profit. In almost all of our cases, these inmates would have to be considered as small-time dealers who would make marginal profits by selling $2-$4 rocks of cocaine to "crack-heads" or to recreational drug-users.

6. Miscellaneous Offenders (14 percent)

   The last group is more difficult to classify, as they fit no particular pattern. Often these individuals have associations with lower-class petty criminals which allows them to periodically become involved in situations that lead to criminal activities and detection by law enforcement.

All these offenders have rather lengthy criminal records. Most have been arrested at least ten times and frequently sentenced to jail, probation, or prison. In this respect, they accurately represent the Habitual Offender label. On the other hand, with the noted exception of the Violent Thugs category, their crimes were petty and pathetic. These are drunken car thieves falling asleep in their victim's car, shoplifters being caught in a clumsy attempt to brazenly walk out of a store with a shopping cart filled with stolen goods, and crack-heads selling

$2 rocks to under-cover agents. They are, in many respects, aging offenders who know no other way to live.

The following five case studies represent a sampling of these offenders. For each, the inmate's offense and sentence is presented along with an estimate of how much money Florida will spend on each individual at today's cost of incarceration ($15,700 per year).

- ALCOHOLIC Alex B—Fraud, Grand Theft, and Burglary—5½ Year Sentence—Incarceration Costs of $64,763.

  Alex is a 46-year-old white male who is spending his first term in prison, although he has 7 prior arrests and one prior jail term. One of his prior arrests and convictions was for assault; the other crimes were non-violent. He has no prior juvenile crime record.

  He is currently serving 3 concurrent sentences for fraud (attempting to pass a bad check worth $20) and entering a person's home wearing a mask and stealing a microwave oven and a TV. He later turned himself in to police. There was no loss to the victim as both items were returned. The victim testified in court that, prior to the offense, Alex had been helping out with various errands and moving furniture. For this crime, he received a 5 year, 6 month sentence for grand theft and burglary. The worthless check crime resulted in a 1 year probation term running concurrently with the burglary and robbery charges. He is also required to pay $200 in restitution to the victim when he is released from prison.

- DRUG DEALER Toni G.—Trafficking Cocaine—Life Sentence—Incarceration Costs of $565,200

  Toni is a 35-year-old African-American female who is serving her third and last time in prison. Under her sentence she must die behind bars. She was caught selling rock cocaine to an undercover police officer in Broward County. There was no violence or injury associated with the crime.

  Toni has been arrested 10 times as an adult, with 7 prior jail sentences. She also has a prior commitment to the juvenile system for being truant. She has no violence in her record. She has four children (ages 16, 13, 12, and 2) who now live with her mother. While on the streets, she was unemployed and made her money running drugs. She completed the 10th grade and has some training as a beautician. While she has tried marijuana, she denied ever using hard drugs. Because of her sentence, she is classified as close custody, but has not received any disciplinary reports since being imprisoned in April 1991.

- VIOLENT THUG Cornelius A.—Arson—12 Year Sentence—Incarceration Costs of $141,300.

Cornelius is a white 37-year-old male who is now serving his fourth prison term. Most of his prior arrests and convictions have been for assault. He has no prior juvenile record.

The current offense involved an attempt to burn down his girlfriend's house as a result of a dispute. He had been drinking heavily at the time. Damage to the house was $1,000 and the only injury was to Cornelius who burned his hand while starting the fire. He was not on probation or parole supervision at the time.

Cornelius is not married, but has 5 children ages 3, 14, 16, and 17 who live with their natural mother (not his current girlfriend). He is functionally illiterate having completed the 5th grade and just now learning to read. He was employed full-time as a maintenance worker at his sister's truck rental business. Since being admitted to prison approximately 1 year ago, he has not been involved in any serious disciplinary incidents and has enrolled in a reading class. He is now classified as medium custody.

- CRACKHEAD Elaine D.—Burglary—15 Year Sentence—Incarceration Costs of $176,625.

Elaine is a 32-year-old African-American female who is serving her second prison term. She has 13 prior arrests for drug and property crimes and has been sentenced to jail 6 times in addition to her 2 prison terms. There has been no violence in her crimes. She was caught trying to break into an apartment, but was apprehended by police after a neighbor called. There was no property loss or damage. She was high on heroin at the time of the crime.

Elaine has been using heroin for many years. She is married to a dope fiend. They have one child—an 8-year-old boy who lives with Toni's sister. At the time of her arrest, she was working full-time as a nurse's assistant and X-ray technician. She has a simple work detail in the prison and has received two disciplinary reports for disobeying orders. She will be released from prison in the year 2003.

- CRACKHEAD Peter A.—Possession and Sale of Cocaine—10 Year Sentence—Incarceration Costs of $117,750.

    Peter is a 50-year-old white male who is serving his fourth prison term. He has a very lengthy adult and juvenile arrest record with three previous juvenile commitments and over 50 adult arrests. There are no violent crimes in his past. He is a drug addict who sells drugs and steals to support his drug habits. His current prison term resulted when police stopped him on the street and found a couple of $5 rocks of cocaine in his possession along with a pipe he used to smoke the crack. He was high on crack at the time of the arrest.

    He has been married to the same woman for 16 years and has three grown children (ages 18, 21, and 25). He is functionally illiterate with a 5th grade education. When not is prison, he finds part-time work as a mason tender or shrimper. Since being imprisoned in 1991, he has not received any disciplinary infractions and has been attending AA and a drug treatment program.

CONCLUSIONS

Our research indicates that most people being sent to prison today are very different than the specter of "Willie Horton" that fuels the public's fear of crime. Most crimes are much pettier than the popular images promoted by those who sensationalize the crime issue. More than half of the persons sent to prison committed crimes that lacked any of the features the public believes compose a serious crime.

Other recent research supports our findings. The original Rand Corporation studies on career criminals that greatly influenced the current imprisonment binge actually found that the vast majority of newly admitted inmates were low-rate offenders involved in petty crimes. When these same researchers studied people they labeled as "high-rate" and "predatory" offenders, their findings were similar to ours—that most in this group committed very unskilled and unprofitable crimes. As Greenwood and Turner note, many high-rate "offenders appeared to have taken foolish risks for very modest potential gains."[22]

Our study revealed that the popular conception of criminal careers is also a distortion of reality. Our data suggest that the majority (57 percent) of the persons sent to prison were not following criminal careers. Although 43 percent were "into crime," most of these (60 percent) were sent to prison for petty crimes, and their dedication to criminal behavior did not appear to be as firm as the popular image suggests. In fact, the majority of them, as well as the majority of those following other patterns of crime (e.g., one-shot, episodes, being around crime, or dereliction), indicated to us that they wanted to stop violating the law and were preparing themselves in prison for conventional careers. As Greenwood and Turner observed, "a much larger proportion of [career criminals] are not particularly successful at crime, but they periodically return to it because they are not good at anything else."[23]

Instead of a large, menacing horde of dangerous criminals, our inner cities actually contain a growing number of young men, mostly nonwhite, who become involved in unskilled, petty crime because of no avenues to a viable, satisfying conventional life. The majority (65 percent) of our arrest samples had not finished high school, 64 percent had no job skills, over half had never been employed steadily, and 56 percent were not working at the time of arrest. The same is not true of a small percent of our sample, who appeared to be committed to crime in spite of other options. In addition, a few were guilty of very serious crimes. However, the general picture is one quite different than the distorted images that have fueled our imprisonment binge.

In 1987, the Bureau of Justice Statistics reported on a national survey of 1,920 U.S. residents. Seventy-one percent had responded that a prison sentence was the most suitable penalty for a group of 24 specific crime scenarios, which included rape, robbery, assault, burglary, theft, property damage, drunk driving and drug offenses. The authors of the report suggested that "the public wants long prison sentences for most crimes." The scenarios, however, did not reflect the reality of street crime and imprisonment in America. In the robbery scenario from the study, for example, $1,000 was taken, the offender brandished a gun, and the victim was hospitalized. Our study discovered that less than 5 percent of the people being sent to prison committed a crime of this magnitude, which we would classify as very serious.[24]

A number of other studies have also discovered that when respondents are given scenarios that are closer to the actual crimes of most people sent to prison, the majority recommend some punishment other than imprisonment. A national poll taken by the Wirthlin Group in 1991 found that four out of five Americans favored a nonprison sentence for offenders who are not dangerous. A 1991 California poll found that three-fourths of Californians felt that the state should find ways of punishing offenders that are less expensive than prison. In Alabama and Delaware, focus-groups analysis conducted by the Public Agenda Foundation found that when citizens were given detailed data about the crimes committed and the relative costs of various sanctions available to the courts, the public strongly supported nonprison sentences for inmates convicted of nonviolent crimes (who represent the vast majority of prisoners).[25] Collectively, these polls show that a majority of citizens would *not* recommend imprisonment for most of the people being sent to prison if they knew more about the offenders' crimes and life circumstances.

NOTES

1. Marvin E. Wolfgang, Robert M. Figlio, and Thorsten Sellin, *Delinquency in a Birth Cohort* (Chicago: University of Chicago Press, 1972).
2. Peter Greenwood and Alan Abrahamse, "Selective Incapacitation" (Santa Monica, Calif.: Rand Corporation, 1982).
3. Peter Greenwood and Susan Turner, "Selective Incapacitation Revisited: Why the High-Rate Offenders Are Hard to Predict" (Santa Monica, Calif.: Rand Corporation, 1987).
4. See Alfred Blumstein, Jacqueline Cohen, and David P. Farrington, "Criminal Career Research: Its Value for Criminology," *Criminology* 26, 1 (February 1988): 1–35, for a summary of their work of criminal careers.
5. Michael Gottfredson and Travis Hirschi, "The True Value of Lambda Would Appear to Be Zero: An Essay on Career Criminals, Criminal Careers, Selective Incapacitation, Cohort Studies, and Related Topics," *Criminology* 24, 2 (1986): 213.

6. U.S. Department of Justice, Bureau of Justice Statistics, "National Judicial Reporting Program, 1988" (Washington, D.C.: U.S. Government Printing Office, 1992).
7. Economic and Demographic Research Division, "An Empirical Examination of the Application of Florida's Habitual Offender Statute" (Tallahassee, Fl.: Joint Legislative Management Committee, the Florida Legislature, August 1992).
8. Tony Fabello, "Sentencing Dynamics Study" (Austin, Tx.: Criminal Justice Policy Council, January 1993).
9. U.S. Department of Justice, Bureau of Justice Statistics, "Historical Corrections Statistics in the United States, 1850–1984" (Washington, D.C.: U.S. Government Printing Office, December 1986).
10. The main reason for choosing these states was access. We wanted to include California, but the then Director of Corrections refused our request. Among those states we had access to, we selected these three on the grounds that they represented a spread on several variables (urban–rural, small population–large population, West–Midwest) and particularly on rates of incarceration.
11. Each selected inmate was informed of the purpose of the interview and was told that participation was voluntary. Only three inmates refused to participate. In those instances in which an inmate declined to participate, his name was replaced with another name from the same crime category list.

    Each prison was visited twice and 25 persons were selected each time. This was done to spread the sampling over a longer time period and thereby avoid any peculiar skewing of the samples by temporal variables. Also, we mistakenly selected and interviewed four persons over the 50 total at Washington. We left them in our study because we eventually adjusted our stratified sample so that our percentages of different crime categories—e.g., robbery, violent, other theft, drug, sex and miscellaneous crimes—corresponded to national percentages. Consequently the four extra interviews did not introduce any distortion.
12. It will be recalled that our original samples were stratified so that each crime category had an equivalent number of prisoners to be interviewed. Given that the vast majority of persons admitted are convicted of property and, increasingly, drug

crimes, our samples had disproportionate numbers of violent crimes and robberies and needed to be statistically adjusted to reflect a true intake population. This was done by reweighting the sampled cases consistent with their observed proportions in the national admission data. For example, offenders convicted of robbery represent 11 percent of prison admissions as compared to the 20 percent representation in our sample. To make our sample nationally representative of robbers, we reweighted the robbery cases by a factor of .55 so that they constitute 11 percent of the adjusted sample.

13. For a review of these evaluations, see Jack Alexander and James Austin, *Handbook for Evaluating Objective Prison Classification Systems* (San Francisco, Calif.: National Council on Crime and Delinquency, 1991).

14. When we adjusted the total sample, we used the national data on percentages of the crime categories. For these state distributions, we adjusted our samples according to each state's offense distribution. Consequently, comparisons between the national estimates and the state specific estimates are somewhat inconsistent. For example, none of the three states has as high a percent of petty crimes as the total sample. This slight discrepancy is simply the result of the inconsistency of the intake offense distribution of the three states with the national offense intake distribution.

15. "Gang-banging" is the term gang members use for engaging in gang violence against other gangs and more generally for belonging to a gang and participating in gang activities.

16. James K. Stewart, Director, National Institute of Justice, U.S. Department of Justice, *NIJ Reports,* Washington, D.C., 1987, p. iii.

17. The number of these cases is so small (six) that little can be made of these descriptive statistics.

18. Criminal Justice Institute, Inc., *The Corrections Yearbook: Adult Corrections,* Salem, NY: Criminal Justice Institute, Inc., 1992.

19. Correctional Association of New York, *Do They Belong in Prison? The Impact of New York's Mandatory Sentencing Laws on the Administration of Justice,* New York, NY: Correctional Association of New York, 1985.

20. Under New York State law, felony murder applies to situations where, during the course of certain designated felonies such as robbery or burglary, the offender's actions result in someone's death. The person charged with felony murder participated in the crime, but did not directly cause the death.
21. James Austin, *Reforming Florida's Unjust, Costly, and Ineffective Sentencing Laws,* San Francisco, National Council on Crime and Delinquency, 1993.
22. Peter Greenwood and Susan Turner, *Selective Incapacitation Revisited: Why High-Rate Offenders Are Hard to Predict* (Los Angeles, Calif.: Rand Corporation, 1987).
23. Greenwood and Turner, p. 36.
24. Press release from the Department of Justice, Bureau of Justice Statistics, Sunday, November 8, 1987. Actually, the Bureau of Statistics was well aware that the scenarios were atypical because an earlier study conducted by them discovered, for example, that the median loss in a robbery was $195 and that 75 percent of all robberies involved less than $700 (J. Frederick Shenk and Patsy A. Klaus, "The Economic Cost of Crime to Victims, Special Report" [Washington, D.C.: Bureau of Justice Statistics, 1984]).
25. See *Americans Behind Bars* (New York: Edna McConnell Clark Foundation, March 1992), and John Doble and Josh Klein, *Punishing Criminals, The Public's View, An Alabama Survey* (New York: Edna McConnell Clark Foundation, 1989).

3

Doing Time

WAREHOUSING PRISONERS

Convicted primarily of property and drug crimes, hundreds of thousands of prisoners are being crowded into human (or inhuman) warehouses where they are increasingly deprived, restricted, isolated, and consequently embittered and alienated from conventional worlds, and where less and less is being done to prepare them for their eventual release. As a result, most of them are rendered incapable of returning to even a meager conventional life after prison. Because most *will* be released within two years, we should be deeply concerned about what happens to them during their incarceration.

Prisons have been called warehouses for decades, but in earlier periods the label was misleading. In most prisons in the first half of the 20th century, prisoners were involved in complex prison societies where they performed all the essential tasks to operate the prison.[1] They cooked and served the meals; washed the clothing; fixed the plumbing, electrical wiring, and appliances; painted the buildings; tended the boiler; landscaped the grounds; delivered most of the medical services; and kept all the records. They worked in prison industries, making "jute," clothes, furniture, license plates, or other commodities consumed by the state. Prison staff oversaw all these activities and kept track of the convicts, but convicts supplied most of the labor.[2]

In addition, convicts played all the sports possible within limits imposed by the physical plant: baseball, football, basketball (when there was a court), handball (there was always a wall for this), boxing, tennis (occasionally there was a court), and even marbles. They carried on the favorite convict pastime, "shucking and jiving"—that is, telling stories about their and others' exploits, mostly in crime, drugs, and sex. They "wheeled and dealed"; they smuggled food from the kitchen and ran sandwich and other food businesses; made prison brew—pruno—which required sugar, yeast, fruit, and some place to stash it during fermentation (a stash was easy to locate, because prunes were such smelly stuff); or bought or sold any contraband that they could steal, smuggle in, or manufacture: food, coffee, stingers (to heat water with), special clothing items, radios, phonographs, typewriters, paper, illegal drugs, even nutmeg (which gives one a cheap high when several spoonfuls are swallowed). Some participated in the special prison sexual life with its "punks," "queens," and "jockers."

Collectively, prisoners developed their own self-contained society, with a pronounced stratification system, a strong convict value system, unique patterns of speech and bodily gestures, and an array of social roles—"right guys," "politicians," "crazies," "regulars," "punks," "queens," "stool pigeons," and "hoosiers." Importantly, their participation in this world with its own powerful value system, the convict code, gave them a sense of pride and dignity. It was them against what they perceived as a cruel prison system and corrupt society.

The prison administration tolerated, even encouraged most of the convict activities and their social organization because these features promoted a high degree of order within the prison. Rarely did the administration have to intervene to maintain control over the inmates. The convicts ran the prison and kept the peace. There was not much emphasis on reformation or "rehabilitation," and most inmates left prison without having improved or acquired skills for living a conventional life. However, society was more accepting of the ex-convict than it is now and apparently most did not return to prison.[3]

THE DEVELOPMENT OF THE CONTEMPORARY PRISON

Immediately after World War II, many state prison systems adopted the rehabilitative ideal and attempted to change their "big house" prisons into "correctional institutions."[4] In the big houses, tough authoritarian wardens watched over populations of prisoners who, for the most part, did their time immersed in the prison society just described. In correctional institutions (which became the new name for prisons), offenders were imprisoned not for punishment but for rehabilitation. During the 1950s and 1960s, prisoners were sentenced under "indeterminate" sentence systems, which granted prison and parole board officials considerable discretion over when an inmate was to be released. Inmates were expected to be involved in a variety of treatment programs and released when parole boards decided the inmate had responded to treatment. However, a variety of factors, particularly the lack of sufficient funds, undermined the delivery of rehabilitation, and consequently the rehabilitation model never was implemented as designed.

The Demise of Rehabilitation. The whole concept of treatment presumed that inmates had deficiencies that could be treated within a prison environment. By the late 1960s and early 1970s, many observers of the rehabilitative penal system began to question this assumption. Specifically, a number of questionable, discriminatory, and even illegal practices were being carried on in the name of rehabilitation and through the margins of discretion given prison administrators within the indeterminate sentence system.[5] Adding to the growing criticism of the rehabilitation model, criminologists who had conducted or reviewed studies found that prison-based rehabilitative efforts in prison did not work.[6] They found that prisoners who participated in a wide range of rehabilitative programs were rearrested at the same rate as those who did not.

Consequently, in the early 1970s, "liberal" reformers sought to abolish indeterminate sentence systems and replace them with the short and uniform sentences known as "determinate" sentencing. In the mid-1970s, as these efforts were beginning to produce some changes in sentencing statutes and policies across the country, conservatives took up the issue of criminal justice and also called for an end to not only the indeterminate sentence systems but all prison rehabilitation. Unlike the liberal-minded reformers, however, conservatives objected to rehabilitation and indeterminate sentencing because inmates were being released too quickly, only to prey again, they insisted, on the public.

As the divergent efforts of liberals and conservative critics both sought to eliminate indeterminate sentencing for different reasons during the late 1970s, public fear of crime rose significantly and conservatives had their way. Most states instituted sentencing and parole policies that made sentences more uniform and considerably longer (mandatory minimum prison laws) for many crimes (e.g., residential burglaries, crimes involving the use of guns or violence, drunk driving, sex crimes, and/or criminals with prior convictions—habitual offenders).[7] In addition, most of the states that shifted their emphasis from rehabilitation to punishment reduced funding for rehabilitative programs, including education and vocational training.

Prison Crowding. As the conservative sentencing agenda took hold, prison populations began to escalate. Though prison construction has proceeded at a rapid rate, it still has not kept up with the prisoner population explosion discussed in Chapter 1. In 1990, only nine states were operating their prisons below their rated bed capacities.[8] Prisons nationwide were overcrowded by a factor of nearly 30 percent. Nine states and the federal prison system reported populations exceeding 150 percent of capacity. These statistics mean that to accommodate the excessive inmate population, cells built to hold one inmate had to be converted to double cells. Similarly, classrooms, gymnasiums, and recreation rooms have been converted to dormitories. Many prisoners are being held in new, rapidly constructed prisons that have only the bare facilities required to house and maintain prisoners.

But these short-term efforts to expand the capacity of existing prisons have not been sufficient to meet the growing need for more prisons. Consequently, most states have embarked on record-level prison construction programs. Between 1989 and 1990, approximately 50,000 beds were added to the nation's prison bed system. Large states like California, New York, and Texas have already spent billions of dollars on prison construction and will require even more billions of dollars to keep pace with the exploding prison population.

In this frenzy of prison construction, states have adopted two strategies for siting new prisons. One approach has focused on expanding the capacity of existing prisons by appending new prisons to existing sites. This strategy is popular because it bypasses the problem of siting prisons in communities where they are not welcomed. The only requirements are open space adjacent to the current prison and water and sewage systems sufficient to handle the additional prison and staff populations. This strategy has resulted in the emergence of megaprisons where 5,000 to 10,000 prisoners can be accommodated at a single site.

The second strategy has prompted many states to return to an old tradition by placing most new prisons in remote areas, far from urban centers.[9] There are three main reasons to do this: land is cheaper and more available in remote areas, most urban and suburban populations do not want prisons in their midst, and many rural communities that are experiencing financial difficulties welcome the economic benefits of a prison, which will provide employment and tax revenues.

There are other consequences to building prisons in remote areas, however. Since the vast majority of prisoners come from cities, this means that relatives and friends visit prisoners at much greater expense and much less frequently (if at all). Also, many fewer organizations, such as schools, churches, unions, businesses, voluntary support groups, are available to offer services to prisoners. These circumstances have greatly increased the isolation and deprivation of prisoners.

Racial Skewing. As noted in Chapter 2, the number of black and Hispanic prisoners continues to grow.[10] In 1923, the first year that the racial makeup of the nation's prison system was counted, 31 percent of the inmates were black. By 1990, that figure had reached 47 percent black, with another 15 percent of Hispanic origin.[11]

Before the 1950s, black and white prisoners were segregated into separate prisons in the South and into separate sections of prisons in other parts of the country. The convict societies in the East, Midwest, and West were dominated by white prisoners, who were a majority, were racially prejudiced, and enforced "Jim Crow" segregation patterns. Formal segregation was ended by the 1960s, and the growing numbers of nonwhite prisoners began asserting themselves, sometimes violently, in prison social affairs. The solidarity of prisoner society was shattered and prisoners divided into hostile factions, mostly based on race and location of residence before prison.[12] Some of these factions are murderous racial gangs that have dramatically altered the prison world.

Court Intervention. In the early 1960s, Black Muslim prisoners in Illinois won a case on their right to follow practices related to their religion. Their successful litigation and a few subsequent cases expanded the remedies available to prisoners under a writ of *habeas* *corpus* and removed procedural obstacles to filing such writs in federal courts, thereby ending the court's "hands-off" policy toward prisoners grieving their treatment in prison.[13] More and more prisoners, inspired and aided by the protest movements of late 1960s and early 1970s, sought remedy for their treatment, and increasingly the courts intervened into the management of prisons. In the late 1970s, the Prison Law Project of the ACLU filed a case in Alabama arguing that the "totality" of conditions in the state's prison system constituted cruel and unusual punishment. The federal court heard the case, held for the complainants, and oversaw the correction of the unconstitutional conditions. Other "in-total" cases have followed. In effect, the courts have moved from "hands off" to active intervention in the management of prisons.[14]

Breakdown of Administrative Solidarity. As mentioned earlier, the big houses before WWII were traditionally run by an authoritarian warden. White rural males, often raised in the small towns near the prison, filled the ranks below this figure of authority. A formal, military-like hierarchy and an informal, good-old-boy social organization with its special guard culture produced a great deal of solidarity among administration and staff.[15]

As states embraced the rehabilitation concept, along with the need to hire more staff for the rapidly expanding prison population, many treatment-oriented administrators and staff were hired or advanced in prison agencies. The influx of personnel with a nonsecurity orientation drove a wedge between the new staff and the old guard, who believed in punishment and maintenance of order. Furthermore, several court rulings on employment hiring practices that had excluded minorities and women resulted in the hiring of more and more nonwhite and female guards. As the size of the correctional system work force increased, it was organized into increasingly powerful labor unions and professional organizations (e.g., American Correctional Association, American Probation and Parole Association), which have become very active in pursuing the interests of their rank and file. Consequently, the top administration has lost a considerable amount of control over its employees, who are now divided along many lines: race, gender, union versus management, and rural versus urban. The prison administration has belatedly followed the path of other government organizations in moving from a more homogenous, informal social organization to a formal and professionalized bureaucracy.[16]

Administrative Confusion. Presently, prison administrators lack a vision to give their task purpose and direction.[17] Rehabilitation, the guiding principle of penology for at least 20 years, has fallen into disrepute. Its replacement, punishment, for administrators converts simply to maintaining order in the prisons. Given the rapidly expanding prison populations, the new problems of keeping prisoners under control, and a more politically active labor force, prison administrators have their hands full dealing with the day-to-day exigencies of running a crowded, unstable, conflict-ridden prison system. In effect, they have evolved from captains of ships to bureaucrats. To cope, they increasingly turn to formal procedures, rules, and standards.

Guards have taken the new emphasis on imprisonment for punishment as a mandate to employ excessively firm, even extreme force to keep prisoners in line, as the following report of a "cell extraction" reveals:

> On Monday, July 2, 1990, at approximately 1710 hours, Inmate Smith refused to relinquish his tray following the evening meal. After numerous unsuccessful attempts were made by the Unit officers and sergeants to retrieve the tray, permission was given by the Administrative Officer of the Day to extract Smith from his cell. At approximately 1730 hours Sergeant Wilson incapacitated Smith with taser round and he was placed in mechanical restraints [handcuffs and leg irons] by an extraction team. Smith was treated by medical staff for minor abrasions and rehoused. There were no injuries to staff. Smith was written up on a 115 and charged with violation of D.R. 300(c), Force and Violence.[18]

The actual result of this encounter, however, was to widen the gap of hostility, hate, and violence between guards and prisoners.

THE BUREAUCRATIC PRISON

The trends noted here have forced states to move from what James Jacobs called a "patriarchal organization based on traditional authority to a rational-legal bureaucracy."[19] This new management style requires a more centralized approach for managing prisons that takes authority and discretion away from the wardens and individual prisons. Directors of corrections now oversee a vast, corporate-like conglomerate of prisons, work release centers, and parole units supported by increasingly sophisticated accounting and computerized information systems. Many of the senior staff who work in the corporate headquarters have no experience in running prisons but have expertise in accounting, information systems, and planning.

The lines of authority, as well as the procedures, prescriptions, or guidelines for all practices, are formalized in the written rules and regulations appearing in elaborate manuals. An extensive and professionalized training program is needed to keep staff abreast of the most recent changes in an increasingly complex array of administrative regulations and procedures imposed by the central office. Routine audits are conducted by central office staff to ensure compliance. In effect, wardens and other key figures in the prison, such as the formerly powerful captain, no longer have the autonomy and wide discretion they once possessed. They must now answer to the central command and do things according to the book.

As the work force has become increasingly professionalized, with college-educated staff who claim to possess special expertise in the area of "corrections," salaries and status have increased correspondingly. In 1991, for example, California prison guards earned an average base salary of $35,016 to $42,552 not including overtime, which can total tens of thousands more dollars each year. By virtue of their work experience alone, they claim a specialized discipline of prison operations and have built a protective wall of esoteric knowledge to justify their actions.[20]

The procedures are based upon ostensibly valid scientific methods or knowledge. For example, "classification" of prisoners for the purpose of assignment to particular prisons, to custody levels they are to be held in, and to "programs," such as educational or vocational training programs, generally involves less discretion and individual judgment than was previously exercised by captains, lieutenants, and guards. Though the policy formation and decision-making procedures are now more centralized, they are also much more subject to outside influences. The intervention of the courts described earlier has meant that many procedures are either court mandated or developed within court-mandated guidelines. In many states, for example, the courts have ordered that minimal due process procedures be followed in all disciplinary actions and that objective classification systems be implemented. And all states must conform to statutes or case law that guarantee certain prisoner rights.

Formerly, wardens and line staff relied mostly on informal systems of control. In most states, prisoner leaders were given power through various informal arrangements and these inmates maintained order in the prison. In many states these prisoners were "right guys" or "politicians" who were given special privileges in return for keeping other prisoners in line. In some southern states, such as Texas and Arkansas, convict "barn bosses" were given the right to control prisoners through intimidation and violence, including homicide. The informal prison social system effectively controlled by "right guys" and "politicians" who were almost always white, disappeared when prisoner populations became increasingly black, Hispanic, and militant. By 1980, most states were required by court intervention to eliminate these convict boss systems.[21]

Bureaucratic professional administrations now attempt to control prisoners through increasingly formal and rational systems. They have promulgated more extensive and restrictive formal procedures and rules governing prisoner behavior and have made greater use of classification and new formal incentives, such as time off for participation in work programs and compliance with prison regulations.

Administrators use three forms of classification. The first is the assignment of prisoners to a custody level that in turn is used to assign them to either a minimum-, medium-, or maximum-security prison. In many states, the committee or classification unit relies heavily upon a quantified "objective" scoring system based on a prisoner's past criminal record, current conviction and sentence length, escape history, and social factors such as age, marital status, and employment history. After the inmate has been in custody for a certain period of time, he or she is reclassified on a different instrument that places greater emphasis on the inmate's record of institutional misconduct.

Interestingly, these new objective classification systems have revealed that the majority of newly admitted inmates require minimum custody since most admitted prisoners have been convicted of a property or drug crime, have no history of violence or escape, have not been to prison before, and will not pose a disciplinary problem for prison officials. Moreover, since most inmates do not become involved in serious disciplinary incidents, they tend to be reclassified to minimum security facilities over time. In many states such as Illinois, California, Florida, Texas, Nevada, and South Carolina, 30 to 50 percent of the average daily population now qualifies for minimum security.

Once the inmate arrives at a facility, a second classification system, often less objective and structured, determines which programs the inmate can participate in and assigns the inmate to a housing unit. Typically, the new bureaucratized prisons have several different sections, such as protective custody and honor cellblocks, to which a prisoner may be assigned. A prisoner's custody level also determines what range of jobs are available to him. For example, minimum-custody prisoners, even at a maximum-security prison, are usually allowed to leave the walled or fenced prison compound to attend to various work assignments: landscaping, working in staff houses on the prison grounds, assisting at the front gate, and the like.

Finally, prisoners who are seen as a threat to the prison social order or to other prisoners are frequently assigned, through another classification process, to highly secure units, where—except for two or three two-hour exercise periods a week, restricted visits, and occasional official business (e.g., talking to their lawyers)—they remain locked in their cells 24 hours a day. In most states, classification to "lockup" (the common general name for these units) includes some limited due process mandated by state or federal courts.

THE PRISONER EXPERIENCE

Inmates in state and federal prisons must presently cope with an extremely aggravating and threatening set of conditions brought on by crowding, racial conflict, new practices stemming from the punitive penological philosophy, and bureaucratic policies. The worst of these features is prisoner-to-prisoner violence.

Violence. As mentioned, prison populations have become much more racially heterogeneous and divided, and the old prison leaders have lost their control over other prisoners. Racial hatred, which often leads to violence, is endemic. Prison gangs attempt to control prison rackets, protect their members, pursue vendettas against their enemies, and earn prestige as "tough" convicts by menacing all other prisoners. In the 1970s and 1980s, assaults and homicides in most high-security prisons became so common that the possibility of being attacked or killed has loomed as the major concern of offenders incarcerated in these prisons or anticipating going to one. Looking at California, where the new prison violence started, prisoner homicides increased dramatically after 1970 (Figure 3-1). They peaked in 1972, with 35 fatalities, 32 by stabbing. The numbers stayed high until the late 1980s and then dropped to reach a low of four. Evidently, California's policy of segregation is reducing prisoner-to-prisoner violence significantly.[22]

> I've been on the yard watching people get shot, watching people die. You know how hard it is coming out with tears in your eyes knowing that you're going to get hit, knowing that someone is going to physically hurt you, or try to kill you . . . 82, 83, 84, people were dropping like flies, people getting stuck. After two or three years of that, it's hard. People on the outside say, ah, that doesn't happen. You weren't there, man.[23]

Prisoners must constantly prepare themselves to cope with this possibility. What they actually do will be discussed later.

Restricted Freedom. Because of prisoner rights statutes and court rulings over the last 20 years, inmates may now receive any publication that may be legally sent through the mail (except those likely to excite violence); correspond and receive visits from many more persons than in earlier eras; enter into contracts, including marriage; receive conjugal visits (when eligible); have a partial due process hearing when they receive punishment within the prison; and are protected from systematic physical brutality delivered by the administration (or their agents, such as the convict bosses). However, only the last of these has substantially improved the prisoner's situation.

Much more important to prisoners is that they have lost much of their physical mobility and access to prison facilities and resources. In earlier years, when prisoners were not working, they were usually allowed to wander relatively freely around the prison facilities: in and out of their cellblock to the yard, gym, library, canteen, and other sections of the prison, such as the school facilities. Now, most maximum- and medium-security prisoners may only make use of these areas and facilities during short designated periods. Most of the time during the

FIGURE 3-1a Number of Fatal Assaults Against Staff and Inmates, 1970–1988

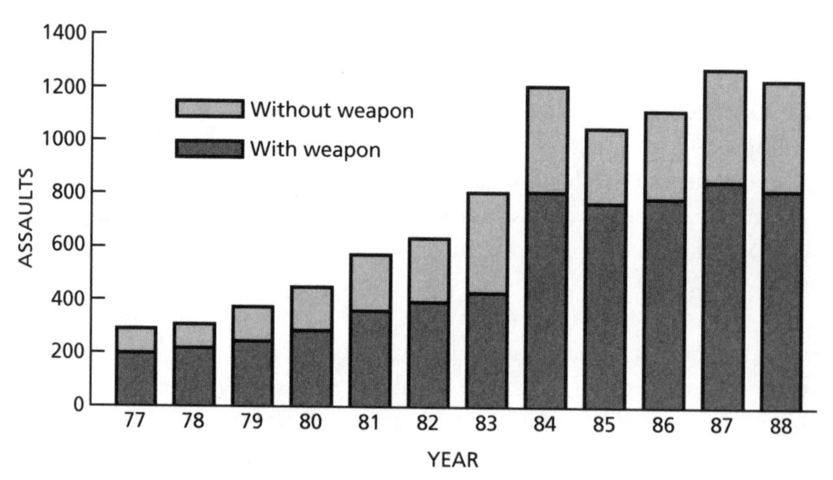

FIGURE 3-1b Number of Inmate Assaults on Inmates, 1977–1988

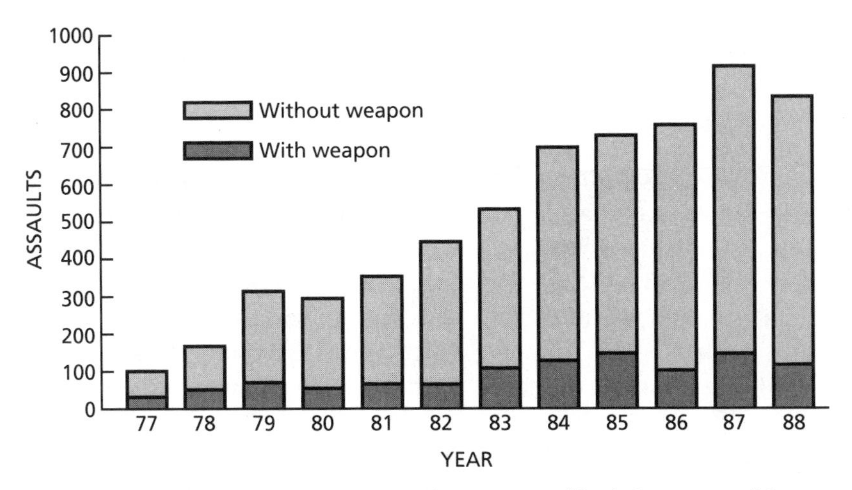

Source: *Behavior of Inmates in CDC Institutions* (Sacramento: California Department of Corrections, 1988).

FIGURE 3-1c Number of Inmate Assaults on Staff, 1977–1988

day and night, prisoners are either at their work or school assignment, or restricted to their cellblock or cell.

Moreover, in most high-security prisons, many prisoners are held in the special lockup units already described. Except for one or two weekly excursions to special exercise yards, an infrequent visit or interview with a prison staff person, prisoners in lockup are in their cells 24 hours a day. (The increased use of maximum security and segregation will be discussed fully in Chapter 4.)

Reduced Resources and Contacts. As a consequence of the redefinition of prisons as locations for punishment (instead of rehabilitation), of overcrowding, and of the new quickly constructed, remote prisons, the resources prisoners may use to accomplish a variety of goals—education, vocational training, and recreation—have dramatically decreased. The states that have expanded their prison populations are driven by punitive sentiments and are usually fiscally conservative. Consequently, the proportion of money for programs and features other than those promoting security have been reduced. Moveover, the remote location of the new prisons has meant that most of the services and support voluntarily offered to prisoners from churches, prisoner support organizations, family, and other individuals have diminished greatly.

Arbitrary Disciplinary Punishment. As mentioned, prison staff must follow a partial due process system in disciplining prisoners. However, prisoners view the due process disciplinary procedure as a sham and much more arbitrary than it was in preceding decades. The "judge" or "judges" in these hearings are prison officials who are far from impartial. In fact, they are often close associates of the persons who bring the charges against the prisoner. Moreover, their primary goal is maintaining order in the prison, not delivering fair, legal, and impartial decisions. In addition, much of the evidence used against the prisoner is hearsay and anonymous—often a "note dropped"; that is, an anonymous letter from a prisoner, sent to the administration through special mechanisms for this purpose. For example, a prisoner at San Quentin was placed in the "hole" (solitary confinement) for participating in a cell burning:

> When I was in the honor block, someone "dropped a note" on me and accused me of being the "point" for a cell burning. I had nothing to do with it, but I couldn't convince 'em in the hearing. I offered to take a lie detector test. They put me in Max B, and I wrote an appeal. After a few weeks, a guy came from Sacramento. Eventually, he arranged for a lie detector test and I passed it. They still left me in the hole for the rest of my sentence.[24]

"Chickenshit Rules." In earlier eras, prisoners enjoyed considerable freedom to embellish their drab and monotonous prison life. For example, they decorated the walls of their cells, altered their prison clothing, acquired various pieces of furniture—such as rugs, chairs, and bookshelves—and kept birds and other small pets in their cells. These special touches enriched their lives with considerable comfort and individuality, which is very important in a world so marked by monotony.

The centralization of authority and the formalization of rules and regulations have resulted in a much more stringent and uniform prison routine that has mostly eliminated these special features and privileges.

Dannie Martin, an ex-prisoner at Lompoc, a federal maximum security prison, writes about the "gulag mentality" of Lompoc's recent wardens.

> As the saying goes, it's the little things that make a house a home. To those of us who face the mind-killing boredom of long prison sentences, small changes take on large significance in this our home-away-from-home. Among the small things that matter most to us here are our routines and perks and possessions. They help to personalize this cold world. . . .
>
> A few years ago—in what convicts now call the good old days—there were said to be two kinds of wardens: those who lean toward punishment and those who believe in rehabilitation. These days, it seems there is only one kind. But the different ways they choose to do their punishing make a great difference to us, the punished.
>
> The warden here at Lompoc from 1982 until 1987 was Robert Christiansen. We who lived here during his tenure called him "Defoliating Bob." He earned that nickname upon his arrival by chain sawing a row of stately and beautiful old eucalyptus trees in our "backyard," trees that for 50 years or more had served as a windbreak about 150 yards from the prison perimeter. Our cell-block view apartments had lost another amenity.
>
> Not long after cutting down the trees, the warden poisoned all the squirrels that convicts enjoyed feeding near the prison fences, then mounted a genocidal war against the cats and raccoons that roamed the prison grounds. He also managed to curtail most of the small liberties enjoyed by the convict population. Before his arrival, we had been permitted to wear our own clothes. Now we were to wear strictly tucked-in and buttoned-up government issue. And our recreational opportunities and food went from bad to worse.
>
> He did away with little niceties like Christmas packages from home and unrestricted telephone access. As he made these changes, he was busy installing electronic grill gates in the hallway so that the prison could be sectioned off in case of emergency. Sheet-metal plates went up over windows with an outside view. . . .

> Defoliating Bob retired last year. One of the first official acts of our new warden, R. H. Rison, was to close down our recreation yard until noon every weekday. Those of us who work on night jobs and ran and exercised in the mornings now sit in gloomy cell blocks watching the sun shine through the window bars. . . .
>
> No sooner did the warden close the yard than we lost our chairs, and that hurt. For as long as most of us can remember, we've had our own chairs in the TV rooms as well as in our cells. There's little enough in here for man to call his own, and over the years these chairs have been modified and customized to an amazing degree—legs bent to suit the occupant, arm rests glued on, pads knitted for comfort. And the final personal touch is always the printing of a name on the back. . . .
>
> A couple months ago, the guards came one day with no warning and confiscated all our chairs. Each of us was issued a gray-metal folding chair, along with a memorandum from the new warden stating that anyone writing on or otherwise defacing these chairs would be subject to disciplinary action.[25]

COPING WITH VIOLENCE

Because racial and gang violence has become increasingly prevalent in some prisons, prisoners in such situations must follow a strategy of doing time that reduces the stress of being robbed, raped, assaulted, or killed by other prisoners.

Gang Banging. Beginning in the 1970s, many prisoners, if they were eligible, have been affiliating with a gang or clique for protection. Younger prisoners, who were members of gangs on the outside or who graduated from youth prisons where they were members of gangs, are automatically eligible. Other potential recruits have to prove themselves.[26] Gang affiliates are either core members or associates. The core members hang around fellow gang members and are very active in the gang's pursuits: robbing other prisoners, dealing drugs, controlling some of the prison homosexuals, and carrying on murderous feuds with other gangs, particularly those of other races. The associates, though they do not participate in the day-to-day activities, remain ready to be called on when some large display of force or some other form of assistance, such as smuggling drugs from one location to another or hiding weapons, is needed. In return, they have the protection of the gang and may circulate much more freely in the prison public places and enjoy some of the fruits of the illegal economic activities of the gangs.

Prison administrators have responded to the gangs by attempting to identify the leaders and core members and place them in the segregation units. In many prisons, these suspected gang members will remain in lockup units for many years. This strategy, however, has not completely stopped gang activities, and assaults and murders of other prisoners and guards continue to occur in the special segregation units.[27] Moreover, unidentified and new gang members carry on the activities on the "mainline" (general prison population). In addition, new prisoners from the same neighborhoods or towns, perhaps members of outside gangs, establish new prison gangs or cliques and continue racketeering and violence in the mainline.

Retired Convicts. A few older prisoners who have spent many years in prisons and have earned good reputations as being tough—usually through their affiliation with one of the gangs—can retire from "gang banging" and circulate freely in the prison with immunity from gang attack. Edward Bunker, in his novel about San Quentin in the 1970s, has accurately depicted this prison pattern.

> So, although Earl was at home, it was in the way that the jungle animal is at home—cautiously. . . . He had no enemies here who posed a threat, at least none that he knew, though some might have been threats if he didn't have the affection of the most influential members of the most powerful white gang and friendship with the leaders of the most powerful Chicano gang.[28]

Withdrawal. The majority, particularly prisoners who are serving their first prison sentences and have not been involved in gangs on the outside, shy away from most prisoners and settings where masses of prisoners congregate and withdraw into small orbits or virtual isolation. Although they may occasionally buy from the racketeers, place bets, or trade commodities on a small scale with other unaffiliated prisoners, they stay out of the large-scale economic activities and dissociate themselves from the violent cliques and gangs. They stick to a few friends whom they have met in the cellblocks, at work, on the outside (homeboys), in other prisons, or through shared interests. Either alone or with their few trusted friends, they go to work and/or attend school or meetings of various clubs and formal organizations that the prison administration allows to exist in the prison. Otherwise, they stay in their cells.[29]

CRIPPLED

The fragmenting of prisoner society, the general physical and social isolation of prisoners, the increased use of segregation, and the elevated level of deprivation, fear, and distress act as socially and psychologically impairing forces on most prisoners.[30] For decades, students of the prison have recognized that the combined factors of being isolated from outside society, subjected to a reduced and deprived routine, and acculturated into a unique "convict" belief and value system work to "prisonize" men and women—that is, convert them into persons equipped to live in prison and ill equipped to live outside.[31] It was this insidious process of prisonization that innovative penologists tried to avoid when they planned the "community corrections" approach in the late 1960s.[32]

Now prisoner administrators and other policy makers have completely abandoned the goal of reducing prisoners' isolation from outside society. They build prisons in the remotest regions of the state with only security in mind and further reduce contacts with outside organizations and individuals through their custody-oriented policies. These practices, along with greatly diminished rehabilitative resources, are producing prisoners who have deteriorated in prison and return to the outside much less well equipped to live a conventional life than they were when they entered.

Inmates enter prison poorly educated, vocationally unskilled, and often suffering from serious physical and psychological problems. Most, particularly at the beginning of their sentences, are desirous of bettering themselves while in prison and improving their chances of living some form of rewarding, viable conventional life when they are released:

> I want to go to school and get a trade. Then when I get out I want to have my kids with me, have a good job so I can support them. I want to get the drugs out of my life. (28-year-old black drug addict convicted of armed robbery and episodically involved in crime)

> I think I will pass up getting involved in the gangs in prison. I'm going to go to school and get me a trade. I want a nice job, paying pretty good, something to keep me busy instead of running the streets. (21-year-old black ex-gang banger episodically involved in crime and convicted of armed robbery)

> I going to go to school and get a job. I'm going to try to get into electronics. I want a job I won't get laid off on. As long as I have a job, I don't get into trouble. When I get laid off, I get into trouble. (18-year-old corner boy who was "around crime" and convicted of possession of cocaine with the intent to deliver)

> When I get out I'm going try to find a job. If I can't find a job, I'll do what I have to do to survive. But I won't do anything violent. I might get a license to sell something. That way you keep some change in your pocket. (26-year-old black petty drug dealer who was "into crime" and convicted of possession of cocaine)

As these statements indicate, many prisoners intended to take care of serious health problems, participate in drug or alcohol programs to deal with their addictions, and in general take advantage of whatever resources exist to better themselves. But these resources for change are less available in today's prisons.

In preceding decades, particularly during the rehabilitative era (1950 to 1965), prison administrators greatly encouraged betterment activities, and they supplied the resources and programs for accomplishing them. Educational opportunities, for example, expanded during this period; by the early 1970s, prisoners could receive a high school education in most prisons and some college credit in many. In addition, most prisons offered a wide variety of vocational training programs. Many forms of counseling were also available. Today, classrooms and vocational training facilities have been transformed into temporary living areas to accommodate the growing prison population.

ALIENATED

The general society has always held convicts in some contempt, but in earlier decades there was a greater willingness to forget their past and, once they had served their time, "give them another chance." In the 1960s, there was a large outpouring of sympathy for convicts, and substantial progress was made in reducing the barriers blocking ex-convicts' reemersion into conventional society.[33] For a short period, ex-prisoners were folk heroes and many strutted around, loudly proclaiming and capitalizing on their ex-convict status. This period ended by the late 1970s, and once again the convict and ex-convict became a widely hated and feared pariah. In recent years, whenever an ex-convict is in the news, the media usually focus negatively on that status. Politicians harp on criminal acts committed by released prisoners. Legislators and policy makers, usually with dramatic public display, have passed laws or established policies against hiring ex-convicts for a growing number of jobs. Consequently, most prisoners are acutely aware that they are among society's leading pariahs, and this awareness has greatly increased their alienation from conventional society.

Finally, in earlier decades most prisoners were somewhat psychologically buttressed by the convict identity. The prisoner society, with its solidarity underpinned by a special world view and code of ethics, not only promoted peace, it greatly bolstered prisoners' self-esteem. Though they were society's outcasts and "losers," they took pride in being "right guys," "regulars," or "real convicts." They endured the deprivation of imprisonment, itself a matter for pride, and responded to their degradation by turning the conventional status system upside down. They viewed average citizens as "squares" whose behavior was petty, corrupt, weak, and hypocritical, and they felt particular contempt for society's representatives to whom they were closest—the guards and prison administrators. Most convicts sincerely believed that they were more honorable than squares.

Now most prisoners not only shy away from other prisoners, they feel contempt for their counterparts as well. A former politically active prisoner, about to be released after serving 20 years, addressed a pre-release class:

> If I catch any convict coming around my neighborhood after I'm released, I'm calling the cops, because I know he is up to no good.

Partly as a reaction to their negative image, some prisoners become "outlaws." These are mainly persons who present themselves as "convicts" in the prison and participate in the rapacious, violent activities of gangs. The outlaw scorns the disapproval of society, reveals no mercy or compassion for others, and remains ready to use violence to protect himself or achieve his ends. An archetypical outlaw, Jack Abbott, describes the type:

> The model we emulate is a fanatically defiant and alienated individual who cannot imagine what forgiveness is, or mercy or tolerance, because he has no *experience* of such values. His emotions do not know what such values are, but *imagines* them as so many "weaknesses" precisely because the unprincipled offender appears to escape punishment though such "weaknesses" on the part of society.[34]

Most prisoners, however, just as they have withdrawn from most prison public activities, attempt to disassociate themselves from the convict identity. But their experience of being held in contempt and having no supporting countervalues is profoundly detrimental. Mainly, it completes their full alienation. This social malady has several separate components: a sense of *powerlessness,* the expectation that one's behavior will not succeed in bringing about the outcomes he seeks; *meaninglessness,* lack of a sense of what one ought to believe; *normlessness,* the expectation that socially unapproved behaviors are required to achieve given goals; *detachment,* the disassociation from the central beliefs and values of the society; and *self-estrangement,* the experience of oneself as alien and unworthy.[35] All these aspects of alienation are cultivated in the contemporary prison milieu, making fully alienated convicts incapable of normal participation in conventional activities. They skulk in and around the edges and crannies of society (like the homeless), unexpectedly lash out at others, escape into drug addiction, or succumb to psychosis or suicide.

The disturbing truth is that growing numbers of prisoners are leaving our prisons socially crippled and profoundly alienated. Moreover, they understand that they will be returning to a society that views them as despicable pariahs. They are also aware that they will have more difficulty finding employment than formerly, and consequently their expectations are low. We will examine how these persons fare on the outside in Chapter 5.

NOTES

1. Starting with Donald Clemmer's *The Prison Community* (New York: Holt, Rinehart and Winston, 1958), social scientists produced an extensive literature on prisoner society as it existed in the decades from the 1930s through the 1960s. A few of the studies are Gresham Sykes, *The Society of Captives* (Princeton: Princeton University Press, 1958); Rose Giallombardo, *The Society of Women* (New York: John Wiley, 1966); David Ward and Gene Kassebaum, *Women's Prison* (Chicago: Aldine, 1965); John Irwin, *The Felon* (Englewood Cliffs, N.J.: Prentice-Hall, 1970); and James Jacobs, *Stateville* (Chicago: University of Chicago Press, 1977).
2. The increase of staff supervision is evidenced by the inmate-to-staff ratios, which ranged from 9 to 11 from 1926 through 1940. Since 1945, however, the ratio has continued to shrink until it reached its lowest level of 2.92 by 1979. See Margaret Werner Cahalan, *Historical Corrections Statistics in the United States, 1850–1984* (Washington, D.C.: Bureau of Justice Statistics, 1986).
3. See Daniel Glaser, *The Effectiveness of a Prison and Parole System* (Indianapolis: Bobbs-Merrill, 1964), chapter 1, for a summary of failure rates of released prisoners. They estimate that in the 1950s and earlier, the rate was about 40 percent.
4. See John Irwin, *Prisons in Turmoil* (Boston: Little Brown, 1980) for a more complete analysis of this shift.
5. The recognition of potential and actual abuses under the rehabilitative ideal began with Francis Allen's *The Borderland of Criminal Justice: Essays in Law and Criminology* (Chicago: University of Chicago Press, 1964). The criticism of rehabilitative routines culminated in *The Struggle for Justice*, written by a "working party" for the American Friends Service Committee, 1971. This book was followed by a series of works in which the "justice model" was offered as an alternative to the rehabilitative judicial and penological systems. See Norval Morris, *The Future of Imprisonment* (Chicago: University of Chicago Press, 1974); Andrew von Hirsch, *Doing Justice: The Choice of Punishments* (New York: Hill and Wang, 1976); and David Fogel, *We Are the Living Proof: The Justice Model for Corrections*, Cincinnati: W. H. Anderson, 1975).

6. In the late 1960s, a series of studies and reviews of studies began to indicate that most of the "treatment" programs practiced in the 1950s and 1960s had no impact on recidivism. This was particularly true of the programs based on personality disorder theories. Even though a small number of programs, particularly those that pursued a learning or cognitive approach, seemed to show some reduction in recidivism, a general consensus formed at this time said that "nothing worked." See particularly Robert Martinson, "What Works? Questions and Answers About Prison Reform," *Public Interest*, 35 (April 1974): 22–54; and Douglas Lipton, Robert Martinson, and Judith Wilks, *The Effectiveness of Correctional Treatment: A Survey of Treatment Evaluation Studies* (New York: Praeger, 1975).
7. For a discussion of this "co-optation," see David Greenberg and Drew Humphries, "The Co-optation of Fixed Sentencing Reform," *Crime and Delinquency* 26 (1980): 206–225.
8. See U.S. Department of Justice, Bureau of Justice Statistics, *Prisoners in 1990* (Washington, D.C.: U.S. Government Printing Office, May 1991).
9. This was the practice from about 1850 to 1950, when prisons were seen as places for banishment. However, during the rehabilitative era, during which more general sympathy existed for prisoners, there was some tendency to build new prisons closer to cities. In the late 1960s, progressive penologists recommended that all prisoners should be held close to urban centers. The idea of "community correctional centers" was advanced, though never actually realized (see Irwin, *Prisons in Turmoil,* chapter 6).
10. Most convicts come from inner-city, lower-class populations. Increasingly, the urban lower class is made up of blacks and Hispanics. The young males in these ethnic groups have extremely high rates of unemployment, in some instances close to 50 percent. While idle, they often become involved in social worlds of deviance and crime (such as using and dealing crack cocaine) that offend and threaten the classes above them, and they are arrested at an astounding rate. Black and Hispanic males have from three to ten times the rate of incarceration as whites.
11. See Margaret Werner Cahalan, *Historical Corrections Statistics in the United States, 1850–1984* (Washington, D.C.: Bureau of Justice

Statistics, U.S. Department of Justice, December 1986), and U.S. Department of Justice, Bureau of Justice Statistics, *Correctional Populations in the United States, 1990* (Washington, D.C.: U.S. Government Printing Office, July 1992).

12. See Leo Carrol, *Hacks, Blacks, and Others* (Lexington, Mass.: Lexington Books, 1974); Jacobs, *Stateville;* and Irwin, *Prisons in Turmoil* for discussions of the conflict between racial groups in prison.
13. See Irwin, *Prisons in Turmoil,* pp. 100–106; Jacobs, *Stateville,* chapter 5; and Ben Crouch and James Marquart, *An Appeal to Justice* (Austin, Tx.: University of Texas Press, 1989), chapters 1 and 8 for discussions of these changes.
14. In fact, the U.S. Supreme Court, in a series of decisions dating back to 1972, has edged back to the hands-off policy. However, many federal and state court judges continue to intervene in the management of prisons. In the mid-1980s, at least 45 states had some aspect of their prison systems under federal court order.
15. See Jacobs, *Stateville;* John Dilulio, *Governing Prisons* (New York: Free Press, 1987); and Crouch and Marquart, *Appeal to Justice* for full discussions of the authoritarian prison regimes.
16. Jacobs (*Stateville*) and Crouch and Marquart (*Appeal to Justice*) traced these shifts in their books on Stateville and the Texas prison systems.
17. The recent study by John Dilulio—*Governing Prisons*—has this confusion as its underlying theme.
18. Reported in Robert Schultz, "'Life in SHU,' an Ethnographic Study of Pelican Bay State Prison," M.A. Thesis: Humboldt State University, April 1991, p. 90.
19. *Stateville,* p. 73.
20. See Jacobs, *Stateville,* and Crouch and Marquart, *Appeal to Justice,* for descriptions of the emergence of bureaucratic regimens.
21. See Crouch and Marquart, *Appeal to Justice,* for a description of the court's elimination of the convict boss system in Texas. Also see Thomas Murton and J. Hyams, *Accomplices to the Crime: The Arkansas Prison Scandal* (New York: Grove Press, 1969), for a description of Thomas Murton's confrontation with the convict boss system in Arkansas.

22. Data on prisoner fatalities were obtained from Offender Information Services Branch, California Department of Corrections.
23. Quoted in Schultz, "Life in SHU," p. 95.
24. Interview, San Francisco, 1981.
25. Dannie Martin, "The Gulag Mentality," *San Francisco Chronicle,* Sunday Punch section, June 19, 1989, p. 5.
26. To be eligible, prospective gang members must be of the same race and sometimes come from the same city, town, or neighborhood. They must also have the respect of the other members. To gain this, they must present the persona of a tough convict who is willing to use violence to protect himself and his associates. The prospects may already have earned this reputation outside or in other prisons. If not, they must earn respect, perhaps by assaulting someone of another race or gang.
27. For example, in 1983 two guards were murdered by members of a white prisoner gang in the lockup sections of Marion, the federal maximum security prison, and one guard was killed by several members of a black gang in a lockup unit in San Quentin.
28. Edward Bunker, *No Beast So Fierce* (New York: W. W. Norton, 1973).
29. In a study of prisons in Ontario, Canada, Edward Zamble and Frank J. Porporino found that more than 40 percent of the prisoners interviewed "stay on their own" and another almost 40 percent confine their socialization to a "few friends." The percent who stay on their own increased to over 50 percent by the time they had served 16 months. Over the span of the study, the percent who spent majority of their optional time in their cell increased from 19.8 to 28.6. It must be noted that these were Canadian prisons and the violence and other pressures are probably not as acute as they are in the United States (*Coping, Behavior, and Adaptation in Prison Inmates* [New York: Springer-Verlag, 1988], p. 117).
30. In their study of Ontario prisoners, Zamble and Porporino did not find that prisoners reported either increases in depression, anger, anxiety, guilt feelings, boredom, and loneliness or increases in depression or anxiety, as measured by standard tests of these variables. The same absence of increases in psychological

"symptoms" or indicators of emotional problems have been found in many other studies (see Zamble and Porporino, *Coping,* for a summary of these findings). However, they are measuring different aspects of the "personality" than those addressed here. We are not suggesting that prisoners are becoming emotionally ill but that they are being converted into a distinct personality type—a prisoner—who may be not be anxiety ridden, depressed, guilt ridden, or even extremely angry. What they become is withdrawn, suspicious, untrusting, and socially unskilled. Zamble and Porporino did find that prisoners withdraw more as they serve their sentence.

31. Donald Clemmer introduced the concept in his seminal study of the prison, *The Prison Community.* Dozens of studies since his have further examined this class of detrimental aspects of imprisonment.
32. See the President's Commission on Law Enforcement and Administration of Justice, *Task Force Report: Corrections* (Washington, D.C.: U.S. Government Printing Office, 1967) and Irwin, *Prisons in Turmoil,* chapter 6.
33. One of the authors, John Irwin, an ex-convict, took great advantage of these changes, finished college, and became a college professor.
34. Jack Abbott, *In the Belly of the Beast* (New York: Random House, 1981), p. 13.
35. See Melvin Seeman, "On the Meaning of Alienation," *American Journal of Sociology* 24 (1944): 783–91.

4

Maximum Security[1]

THE HISTORY OF ADMINISTRATIVE SEGREGATION

Prison authorities are placing more and more inmates in "administrative segregation," "maximum security," "control" or "lockup" housing units.[2] These units are unique in granting prison administrators total physical control over all aspects of the inmate's behavior. Inmates assigned to such housing areas spend 22 to 23 hours a day in their single, high-security barren cells with minimal (if any) access to educational, religious, or other self-help programs. Access to small and self-contained razor-wired recreation and exercise "cages" is made available on a very limited basis, with no more than two to three inmates at a time allowed out on the yard. In general, these facilities represent the bottom end of a state's prison system. This trend should concern us greatly because it has many undesirable consequences for prison systems, for prisoners who experience long periods of lockup, and for the society that must receive most of these prisoners back when they are released.

The concept of administrative segregation grew out of the practice of solitary confinement, which prison administrators began using in the last century along with many other methods (such as flogging, water torture, shackling of prisoners to cell walls) to punish particularly troublesome prisoners. By the turn of the century, prison authorities had eliminated most of the other crueler forms of punishment but continued to confine prisoners in "solitary" or the "hole" as the major form of punishment for rule breaking. In his 1940 study of a "prison community," Donald Clemmer described solitary confinement:

> The twenty-four solitary cells are in a small building known as the yard office. . . . "Solitary" is set off by itself and is heavily barred and isolated. The cells themselves contain no furniture. The one window is small, and the iron bars of the door have another wooden door which keeps the light from entering. The cells are cold in winter and hot in summer. The inmate is given one blanket and must sleep on a wooden slab raised about two inches from the cement flooring. One piece of bread and a necessary amount of water is allowed each day.

During the first half of this century, all walled prisons had solitaries or holes. Some, such as the tin sweat boxes in southern work camps or the "dungeon" in San Quentin, were extremely cruel places. The cells studied by Clemmer at the Illinois Menard maximum security prison were about average. During this time, many prisons also had cells set aside for segregation of prisoners—such as persons who persistently broke the rules, open homosexuals, and persons who needed protection from others—whom the administration believed could not be allowed to circulate freely among other prisoners. Unlike solitary confinement, inmates could be held in segregation for long periods of time, sometimes years.

By the 1950s, the old system of social order based on a convict code and a few prisoner leaders was breaking down and new problems of disorder among prisoners developed. Consequently, states began developing new forms of administrative segregation to control an increasingly disruptive inmate population. Many states that had adopted the rehabilitative philosophy of penology—such as California, Illinois, New York, New Jersey, Wisconsin, Washington, and Minnesota—were able to gain conformity for a few years (1950–1955) through the indeterminate sentencing system. Using the margins of sentencing discretion contained in the indeterminate sentencing system along with systems of good-time credits inmates could earn to reduce their prison terms, prison officials and parole boards threatened prisoners with longer lengths of stay if they did not conform in prison. However, a small percent of the prisoners were responsive neither to these sentencing incentives nor to the threat of being placed in the hole. In particular, youthful leaders of well-organized street gangs who had received lengthy prison terms for violent crimes began to assume a greater presence in maximum-security prisons. Prisoner administrators then expanded the use of administrative segregation to manage this growing and difficult-to-manage population.

By 1970, California had established so-called high-security "adjustment centers" at its major maximum security prisons of San Quentin, Folsom, and Soledad.[3] In Illinois, special program units or SPUs were established at Joliet, Stateville, and Pontiac prisons in 1972. Other states soon followed these states in their efforts to isolate and control the most disruptive or potentially disruptive segments of the inmate population.

When these first adjustment centers failed to reduce the turmoil and violence, more sections of several prisons were converted into new segregation units (e.g., "segregated housing units" and "management control units"). By 1980, for example, California had more than 2,000 prisoners in some form of lockup, representing nearly 10 percent of the entire prison population.[4]

THE OFFICIAL PROGRAM

Prisoners are "assigned" (not sentenced) to "segregation" for their perceived status—such as being an ongoing threat to prison stability, staff, and other prisoners. This means that they are not necessarily charged with any specific rule violations and that the assignment does not require any disciplinary procedures, which now, after several court decisions, involve some limited due process. Administrators, therefore, can exercise almost unrestricted discretion in assigning prisoners to a lockup unit.

Additionally, since the official purpose of segregation units is not punishment, the prison administrators initially planned the units' physical structure and routines so that they would not have any special punitive aspects. When expanded use of segregation first began, the cells in segregation units were different than those in solitary units.

They usually had the same furnishings as mainline cells—a bunk, mattress, toilet, washbowl, and sometimes a small desk. Moreover, the prisoners were not intentionally denied other privileges beyond those that were impractical to deliver because the prisoners were restricted to their cells. Lockup prisoners could receive and keep about the same range of material and commodities as mainline prisoners. They either were allowed TV sets in their cells or could watch a TV mounted in the unit. Their mail was not restricted. They received and kept books (although their access to the prison library was and is greatly restricted because of their lockup status).

THE REALITY OF LOCKUP

Lockup status was inherently highly punitive from the outset. In the typical routine of a lockup unit, prisoners were confined to their cell almost 24 hours a day. Officially, they were supposed to spend one or two hours twice a week in a small exercise yard adjacent to their unit, which had limited recreational facilities. In actual practice, these periods were frequently denied prisoners. They were occasionally escorted, sometimes by two to four guards, to other parts of the prison to go to the hospital, a visit, or other special functions (e.g., disciplinary hearings). Otherwise they stayed in their cells.

Most important, being locked up in segregation meant prisoners lost access to most programs and activities, which in most prisons are extensive: schooling, vocational training, movies, libraries, and recreational activities. They were cut off from socializing with other prisoners during work, dining, on the yard, and in the day rooms, and from engaging in literally dozens or hundreds of games, hustles, rackets, and other cooperative enterprises that prisoners undertake. They did talk to each other through the barred fronts of their cells and even played games, such as chess, on the walkway directly in front of their cells. For all intents and purposes, however, prisoners in lockup units were cut off from the general, relatively full social life of the prison world—which, as emphasized in Chapter 3, was often rich and varied.

It is true that this also meant these prisoners were somewhat protected from hostilities and assaults that were increasingly occurring among mainline prisoners. What they sacrificed for this increase in safety, however, was tremendous. Moreover, hostility and violence eventually became more intense in the lockup units than on the mainline.

Turmoil in Lockup. During the 1970s and early 1980s, the segregation units became extremely tumultuous and violent. This was partly a result of the administrative practice of concentrating the most recalcitrant prisoners in the prison system in a situation of relatively severe deprivation. Many of them had not conformed to the rules in the much less restrictive mainline and were even less willing to do so in segregation.

Prison administrators began locking up suspected members of organizations believed to be a threat to prison order. Suspected leaders of the Black Muslims were the first to be segregated, followed by other black religious and political organizations, such as the Black Panther Party. When organizations of other prisoners—Chicanos, whites, and Puerto Ricans—appeared, the suspected leaders were assigned to segregation. In the 1970s, gangs of prisoners of the same race involved in rackets and violence toward other gangs and individual prisoners became the main concern of prison administrations, and all suspected leaders and many suspected members were isolated in the lockup units.

Making matters worse, many prisoners believed that they had been unfairly placed and held in the segregation units. As we have seen, placement was an administrative decision by a "classification committee" that involved minimal due process and at best a pro forma appearance by the inmate at the classification hearing. When Illinois began using its SPUs in 1972, for example, hundreds of inmates were "reclassified" for the Joliet SPU during a single weekend. Inmates were "heard" in hearings that lasted less than a minute.

Once assigned to these segregation units, prisoners' "cases" were reviewed again in a cursory manner. Frequently, the classification committee based its decision on hearsay information, such as that supplied by informers, sometimes anonymously, or suspicions, such as those expressed in memos from staff who reported that they had witnessed prisoners engaging in acts that suggested the prisoners had been involved in some prohibited behavior. Even if an inmate had not been involved in any disciplinary actions, he could remain in the units simply because of staff suspicions.

For these reasons, lockup units became centers of turmoil. Prisoners engaged each other and guards in constant verbal attacks. A prisoner described his experiences on entering one of the first adjustment centers in California:

> [We] were transferred to Soledad Correctional Facility from X Prison. We were placed in the Max Row section, O wing. Immediately entering the sallyport area of this section I could hear inmates shouting and making remarks such as, "Nigger is a scum low-down dog," etc. I couldn't believe my ears at first because I know that if I could hear these things the officers beside me could too, and I started wondering what was going on. Then I fixed my eyes on the wing sergeant and I began to see the clear picture of why those inmates didn't care if the officials heard them instigating racial conflict. The sergeant was, and still is, Mr. M., a known prejudiced character towards blacks. I was placed in a cell, and since that moment up 'till now, I have had no peace of mind. The white inmates make it a 24-hour job of cursing black inmates just for kicks, and the officials harass us with consistency also.[5]

Racial hostilities ran high in these units since they were filled with inmates representing most of the prison gangs. In Illinois, the dominant prison gangs—such as the Black P. Stone Rangers, Black Disciples, Vice Lords, and Latin Kings—were constantly warring with one another for control. In California, the Aryan Brotherhood, Black Guerrilla Family, the Mexican Mafia, and La Nuestra Familia were strongly committed to attacking members of rival groups. When the opportunity presented itself—such as when members of opposing groups were released together to the exercise yard—prisoners fought, knifed, and killed each other. In 1970, a fight between several white and black prisoners housed in Soledad's O Wing broke out as soon as the blacks and whites in the section were released together to the exercise yard. A gun tower guard fired at the prisoners and killed three black prisoners.

Prisoners often broke up their cell furnishings—the beds, cabinets, toilets. On these occasions, water ran out of the cells down the tiers onto the floors. Often the floors in the cells were littered with trash thrown from cells and water running out of cells. To regain order, staff would shoot tear gas into the units and use "stun guns" or "tasers" to subdue inmates. In return, prisoners in lockup units constantly taunted and vilified their guards. They regularly threw any liquid material, sometimes urine and feces, on passing guards and occasionally assaulted and murdered them.

Not surprisingly, as these conditions worsened in adjustment centers, guards grew more hostile toward the prisoners. They were deeply offended and angered by the revolutionary rhetoric delivered by some of the more politically oriented prisoners, in which guards ("pigs" or "the police") were excoriated. For example, George Jackson, who was held in adjustment centers most of his 20 years in California prisons, wrote in 1970:

> The great majority of Soledad pigs are southern migrants who do not want to work in the fields and farms of the area, who can't sell cars or insurance, and who couldn't tolerate the discipline of the army. And, of course, prisons attract sadists.
>
> Pigs come here to feed on the garbage heap for two reasons really, the first half because they can do no other work, frustrated men soon to develop sadistic mannerisms; and the second half, sadists out front, suffering under the restraints placed upon them by an equally sadistic, vindictive society. The sadist knows that to practice his religion upon the society at large will bring down upon his head their sadistic reaction.[6]

The guards' hate deepened when lockup prisoners increased their verbal taunts, began throwing objects and liquid on them, and occasionally succeeded in murdering them. Guards occasionally responded by punishing and harassing prisoners in every way they could. They delivered their own taunts and vilification, occasionally beat prisoners and frequently shortened, disrupted, or denied privileges, such as correspondence, exercise, and visits, that lockup prisoners were supposed to receive. Evidence of these practices was obtained in 1975 by the federal district court investigating the conditions in lockup units:

> Two guards who used to work in the AC testified in support of plaintiffs' allegations that guards have beaten, threatened, and harassed plaintiffs and other first tier AC prisoners, that prisoner reports are at times altered, and that AC guards have a stereotyped view of plaintiffs and treat them in a dehumanizing fashion.[7]

Some guards entered into the conflicts between prisoner factions by aiding one group of prisoners against others or "setting up" individual prisoners. Occasionally, this was done in a routine fashion. For example, a white prisoner who was identified as being affiliated the Aryan Brotherhood described his setup by a black guard:

> This black guard was escorting me back to my cell in Max B [a section of the Adjustment Center] and he stopped and handcuffed me to the rail on the row housing black prisoners and said he would be right back. Then he went and unlocked the row to let all the black dudes out to exercise. As they passed by me, they kicked me, spit on me and punched me. Then he came back and put me in my cell.[8]

Sometimes guards set prisoners up to be killed or even participated in the homicides. In the fight and killings in the Soledad adjustment center yard, in which three black prisoners were shot to death, a Salinas, California jury found that eight Soledad staff members had willfully and unjustifiably conspired to kill the three prisoners. The staff had released prisoners who were expected to begin fighting. The gun tower guard, who some prisoners report was leaning out of his tower aiming at the prisoners when the fight began, fired five shots and hit the three black prisoners in the middle of their torsos. Afterward, the guards took over 30 minutes to carry one mortally wounded prisoner to the hospital even though it was adjacent to the adjustment center.[9]

Guards and the administration steadily reduced the old privileges of the adjustment centers until the distinction between the former punitive solitary units and the nonpunitive adjustment centers had all but disappeared. A psychiatrist, appointed by the Northern California federal district court to examine the AC unit in San Quentin in 1980 commented on the conditions:

> When I walked through Security Housing Unit 2 at San Quentin and heard constant angry screaming and saw garbage flung angrily from so many cells, I felt like I was in a pre-1793 mental asylum, and the excessive security itself was creating the madness. . . .
>
> While the mainline playing fields at San Quentin are large and grassy, the various security units are small and paved. . . .

> Prisoners are not allowed any furniture (desks, chairs, etc.) and are prevented by regulations from even draping their cells with blankets to improve insulation against cold winds. Deprived of most expectable human means of expressing self, prisoners are left with a meager token of wall decorations.[10]

Instead of being locations where prisoners were incapacitated and pacified in a controlled but humane setting, the lockup units became the most dangerous (for both prisoners and staff), punitive, and deleterious settings in American prisons. Robert Slater, who worked at San Quentin as a psychiatrist between 1982 and 1984, describes the violence in that prison's adjustment center:

> Periodically, bursts of gunfire serve as unpleasant reminders of where we are. Occasionally, a prisoner is killed, maimed, or blinded by gunshot. . . .
>
> Crude but effective spears, bombs, hot or corrosive liquids can, and are, hurled through the bars in either direction. In the summer of 1984, during a particularly violent period, the authorities in one of the lockup units brought together a Mexican leader and a Black leader, asking them to walk the tiers together to help cool things down. They agreed to do this. While walking the tiers a Mexican inmate threw a knife through the bars to the Mexican leader, who proceeded to kill the Black leader.[11]

NEW MAXIMUM-SECURITY PRISONS

The apparent failure of administrative segregation units to pacify prisoners and restore order to the prisons during the 1970s and early 1980s did not cause penologists to abandon the policy of concentrating troublesome prisoners in permanent lockup units. What they have done instead is to construct new "maxi-maxi" prisons in which they have attempted to eliminate the features believed to have caused the breakdown of order.

In fact, this goal was first attempted by the Federal Bureau of Prisons when they took over Alcatraz Island, the cite of an old army prison, and opened a small, maximum-security federal prison in 1934.

Alcatraz was intended to house the most "desperate criminals" (e.g., "Machine Gun" Kelly and Al Capone) and the bureau's most troublesome prisoners. By the early 1960s, the feds, particularly the attorney general, Robert Kennedy, considered the "Rock," which housed only 275 prisoners, an expensive failure and closed it in 1963. Its prisoners were dispersed among the other federal prisons, mostly Atlanta and Leavenworth, the two securest prisons next to Alcatraz.

At this time, the Federal Bureau of Prisons was constructing a new small prison at Marion, Illinois, as an experiment in behavior modification. The prison had a range of units with varying degrees of security. About 350 prisoners were supposed to work their way through the levels, increasing their privileges by demonstrating good conduct.

In 1973, however, the FBP returned to the policy of concentrating their troublesome prisoners in one place and began transferring them to Marion's "control unit."[12] The feds continued to send more troublesome prisoners to Marion and reclassified it in 1979 as their only "Level 6" (highest-security) penitentiary, designated for prisoners who

1. Threatened or injured other inmates or staff.
2. Possessed deadly weapons or dangerous drugs.
3. Disrupted "the orderly operation of a prison."
4. Escaped or attempted to escape in those instances in which the escape involved injury, threat of life, or use of deadly weapons.

Since its complete conversion to a prison for problem inmates, Marion has experienced difficulties very similar to those in California's lockup units. Through the 1970s, tensions, hostilities, violence, and disruptions increased. In the early 1980s, the unrest reached new heights. From February 1980 to June 1983, there were 54 serious prisoner-on-prisoner assaults, eight prisoners killed and 28 serious assaults on staff.

The turmoil escalated further in the summer and autumn of 1983. In July, two prisoners took two officers hostage in the disciplinary segregation unit; one officer was stabbed. In the following week, two inmates attacked two officers escorting prisoners from the dining hall. Prisoner-to-prisoner violence increased in this period, and most of the time the prison was placed on complete "lockdown" status. On September 5, a prisoner assaulted an officer with a mop wringer and a chair. On October 10, an officer was assaulted when he tried to break up an attack by prisoners on another prisoner. On October 22, when three officers were moving a prisoner housed in the control unit, the prisoner stopped to talk to another inmate in a cell, then turned to face the officers, his handcuffs unlocked and a knife in his hands. He succeeded in murdering one officer.

That evening another prisoner was being escorted by three officers from one section of the prison to the recreation cage. He too stopped in front of another prisoner's cell and turned around with his handcuffs removed and a knife in his hands. He succeeded in stabbing all three officers, one fatally. The turmoil in the prison continued for another month. Prisoners started fires, threw trash out of their cells, and continued to assault other prisoners and staff. Repeated searches produced weapons, handcuff keys, lock picks, hacksaw blades, heroin, and drug paraphernalia.

The FBP finally instituted new severe control procedures. David Ward and Allen Breed, who conducted a study of Marion for the U.S. House of Representatives, describe the clampdown:

> New custodial procedures were implemented. All correctional officers were issued riot batons and instructed to carry them at all times. A special operations squad, known as "The A Team," arrived from Leavenworth and groups of Marion officers began to receive training in techniques of conducting forced cell moves and controlling resistant inmates. These officers were outfitted with helmets, riot control equipment and special uniforms. A new directive ordered that before any inmate left his cell he was to place his hands behind his back near the food tray slot in the cell door so that handcuffs could be placed on his wrists and leg irons on his ankles. No inmate was to be moved from his cell for any reason without a supervisor and three officers acting as an escort. Digital rectal searches were ordered for all inmates entering and leaving the Control Unit along with strip searches of inmates before and after visits with the attorneys.[13]

As was the case in California and Illinois, strategies to control troublesome prisoners greatly increased control problems.

Because Marion had not been designed to hold the most troublesome prisoners, many of its features, such as open cell fronts, turned out to present problems to the staff in their attempts to maintain complete control over recalcitrant prisoners. Many states are building new maxi-maxi prisons that are designed specifically to hold recalcitrants. In general, these prisons are built to hold prisoners in small, secure, self-contained units. Ward and Breed, in commenting on the inadequacy of Marion's design, describe this type of prison:

> New generation prisons are generally comprised of 6 to 8 physically separated units within a secure perimeter. Each unit of some 40–50 inmates, all in individual cells, contains dining and laundry areas, counselling offices, indoor game rooms, a wire enclosed outdoor recreation yard and a work area. The physical design of inmate rooms calls for only one or two levels on the outdoor side(s) of the unit to facilitate, from secure control "bubbles," easy and continuous staff surveillance of all areas in which inmates interact with each other and with staff.[14]

In addition, the cells in new maxi-maxi prisons usually have solid doors with a shatterproof glass window and an opening through which prisoners can be fed or handcuffed without opening the door.

The basic idea is that prisoners, while being held in small secure units and unable to congregate or communicate with each other, can be delivered all essential services (e.g., food and medical services). This would avoid the problems administrators encounter when they "lock down" an older prison, which greatly disrupts the delivery of essential services to prisoners. In addition, when prisoners in the new maxi-maxi prisons are kept in their cells, they cannot throw things, yell to each other, or assault guards, as is the case in the older prisons, even in the segregation units.[15]

California has become the leader in the construction of super-maximum prisons. It has built four new maxi-maxi prisons with a total capacity of 12,000. Other such prisons have been constructed in Nevada, New Mexico, Texas, and Minnesota, with many more planned for other states and cities with major jails (including Los Angeles, New York, and Philadelphia).

The four California maxi-maxi facilities have some common design features. All have "units" or "pods" that cluster around a central control center from which heavily armed guards look down on the units 24 hours a day. The cells have fully sealed front doors to restrict the throwing of objects by inmates at staff. Each unit typically has a small day room and adjacent exercise yard.

Pelican Bay facility, the last of the four to open, is located in an extremely remote area of Northern California. Built in 1990 at a cost of $278 million, it was designed to hold 2,080 maximum security inmates, but it is already overcrowded with an inmate population of 3,250. Within the prison itself the segregated housing unit has the capacity for 1,056 prisoners:

> Pelican Bay is entirely automated and designed so that inmates have virtually no face-to-face contact with guards or other inmates. For 22½ hours a day, inmates are confined to their windowless cells, built of solid blocks of concrete and stainless steel so that they won't have access to materials they could fashion into weapons. They don't work in prison industries; they don't have access to recreation; they don't mingle with other inmates. They aren't even allowed to smoke because matches are considered a security risk. Inmates eat all meals in their cells and leave only for brief showers and 90 minutes of daily exercise. They shower alone and exercise alone in miniature yards of barren patches of cement enclosed by 20 feet high cement walls covered with metal screens. The doors to their cells are opened and closed electronically by a guard in control booth. . . .
>
> There are virtually no bars in the facility; the cell doors are made of perforated sheets of stainless steel with slots for food trays. Nor are there guards with keys on their belts walking the tiers. Instead, the guards are locked away in glass-enclosed control booths and communicate with prisoners through a speaker system. . . .
>
> The SHU (Segregated Housing Unit) has its own infirmary; its own law library (where prisoners are kept in secure rooms and slipped law books through slots); and its own room for parole hearings. Inmates can spend years without stepping outside the Unit.[16]

California's Governor George Deukmejian, dedicating the new prison in June 14, 1990, stated:

> California now possesses a state-of-the-art prison that will serve as a model for the rest of the nation. . . . Pelican Bay symbolizes our philosophy that the best way to reduce crime is to put convicted criminals behind bars." The Governor also noted that the

> annual cost of keeping a convicted felon in prison is $20,000 compared with the $430,000 that it costs society when a career criminal is at work on the street.[17]

This unit is the most completely isolated prison since the early penitentiaries in Pennsylvania. Since 60 percent of the inmates housed at Pelican Bay are from the Los Angeles area, which is 900 miles away with no available air transportation, the prospect for regular visits from inmates' families is extremely remote. But California is not the only state constructing such units. Oklahoma's new "high-max" unit was described in this way:

> Inmates housed in the "high-max" security unit will live 23 hours a day in their cells, with the other hour spent in a small concrete recreation area with 20-foot walls. The space is topped by a mental grate.
>
> Theoretically, an inmate could move into the new cellhouse and never again set foot outdoors. The unit's first residents will be the 114 men on death row. The cellhouse also contains a new execution chamber.
>
> That's how the staff designed it. For about 45 days, workers representing a cross-section of the penitentiary's staff developed plans for the new unit with architects. Guards in the control room of each squad can eavesdrop on or talk to inmates in any cell at the touch of a button. Fields said the monitoring device should reduce the number of attacks on prisoners, nip conspiracies in the bud and protect officers.
>
> A corridor behind each cell run will allow officials to work on or shut off water and power to each individual cell.[18]

Finally here is a description of New York's new super-max, as reported in *The New York Times:*

> The New York prison Southport Correctional Facility has the same mission: to take the worst prisoners. They will include those who have dealt drugs behind bars, attacked guards, even murdered inmates. At Southport, they are being kept isolated, shackled at the waist and wrists when allowed out of their 6 by 10 foot cells and made to spend their daily recreation hour in newly built cages.[19]

THE CONSEQUENCES OF LOCKUP

It is far from clear that the expanded use of lockup has made prisons easier to manage. It is clear, however, that lockup has a very negative effect on the prisoners who experience long periods of isolation in the various lockup units.

The Self-fulfilling Prophecy. When persons are treated as having certain characteristics, whether they actually have them or not, they are likely to develop such characteristics or have them magnified because of the treatment. This phenomenon frequently occurs when persons are classified as recalcitrant and placed in lockup units. Many persons who have been minor "troublemakers," or who are mistakenly believed to be intensely or intimately involved in prohibited activities (such as revolutionary or gang activities), have been placed in the lockup units and then have actually fulfilled the prophecy—that is, they have become serious troublemakers, committed revolutionaries, or gang members.

Several processes accomplish this transformation. In the first place, many persons are instilled with considerable frustration, anger, and a sense of injustice when they believe they have been unfairly placed in lockup. As mentioned earlier, the process of classifying persons to lockup is often based on hearsay information of dubious reliability. Administrators have always felt a great need to cultivate and rely on information supplied by informers, and they have regularly accepted anonymous information ("notes dropped") and often coerced many persons into supplying information on others. For example, administrators have usually required a prisoner who is seeking protection or is trying to drop out of a gang to name persons who were threatening him or were involved in prohibited activities, such as gang activities. They also have offered such significant incentives to informers as transfers, letters to the parole board, placement in protective custody.

Though some of the information supplied by informers has been reliable, much has not.[20] What occurred simultaneously with the new forms of disruption that prison administrations have been trying to control through the use of informants was the loss of cohesion among prisoners and a weakening of the convict code, which dictated, above all, not to snitch. A new ethic has emerged and guides many prisoners based on the general principle of everyone for himself, or "dog eat dog." Informing for self-gain is consistent with this new code and has become much more commonplace. Even falsely accusing persons for self-advantage is a practice approved of by many prisoners. For example, a prisoner who was transferred from Soledad to San Quentin's segregated housing unit claimed to have been the subject of false accusations by an informer:

> I had this good gig, disc-jockey on the prison radio, and this black dude wanted my job. So he told them that I was active in the AB [Aryan Brotherhood]. I wasn't. I got a lot of friends who were AB. But I've never been AB. I played a lot of Western music, and lot of people didn't like that and didn't like me. The rat who snitched me out of the job didn't like my music. But really he wanted to replace me. So he told the man I was an active AB.[21]

In making their decisions to segregate, the committees also regularly accept staff observations of questionable validity. The following is an example of many statements from memos in files of persons assigned to lockup because of gang affiliations:

> I observed inmate A talking to inmates B, C, and D on many occasions. They seem to have been involved in gang type activities together.[22]

The highly discretionary and arbitrary nature of the gang designation is revealed in the following California correctional officer's description of the process:

> There's three, four, five different ways that they can be designated as a gang member. They're either northern or southern Mexicans just by birth. If they're from south of Bakersfield, they're going to be southern unit. If they're from north of Bakersfield, they're going to be Nostra [Nuestra] Familia. And that's just something that doesn't change. Now after that, you get associations. If for example, we're talking about Nostra Familia, and that's the northern gang, and there's an inmate you know associates, has been observed by staff who's seen writings

> in his letters, if you can use two of the five or six different methods of validation, then you can call him an associate. Letter writing, another inmate telling you, admission of the inmate himself, staff observation, there's several ways to observe and two of the five or six different ways, I believe is, will validate him as an associate. Then to be validated member, then I think it's four out of five or six, you have to be observed by staff, have another inmate tell you, through incriminating himself, he can tell you. Now, you may never ever take any of these vows or do any of their footwork or anything, but just because you hang with people from where you come, you associate with them. Once you've been validated as an associate, or validated as a member, then they can give you indeterminate SHU term.[23]

Consequently, many persons who have had minor behavior problems in prison or have had a weak or no affiliation with some of the organizations suspected of engaging in extremely rapacious, violent, and disruptive behavior have been placed in lockup units.

Once in the lockup units, the prisoners experience the ordinary deprivations inherent in lockup status and frequently witness or are subjected to the additional abuse that results from lockup guards expressing their extreme racism and general hostility toward lockup prisoners. This harassment further enrages many prisoners:

> One day when I got back from the visiting room, inmate M told me that the police had attacked W, a black inmate, while being handcuffed and taken to isolation. We protested according to their ways, and we threw some liquid on officer D, since he was the cause of W getting attacked. They came back and threw tear gas into our cells until we almost died—seriously—I had to wave a towel since I was choking from the gas. They told me that they wouldn't open the door until I got undressed, backed up to the door and stuck my arms out. I did just that. They handcuffed me and dragged me to the other side naked.[24]

In addition, the policy in California prisons throughout the 1970s and early 1980s was to locate suspected gang members in sections designated for a particular gang. This practice often forces persons with weak or no affiliation closer to the gang. First, placing inmates in the unit with a particular gang results in their being viewed as a definite member of that gang and subjects them to the threats and attacks of other rival gangs. Second, if they are accepted by the other gang members, the dynamics of being held in close, exclusive interaction with these others strengthens the bonds between them. Consequently, weak or no affiliation is often converted to full membership by the lockup decision.

"Monsters." "They treat me like a dog, I'll be a dog."[25] Many persons held for long periods in lockup, during which they have been subjected to extreme racial prejudice, harassment by the guards, and threats and attacks from other prisoners, are converted into extremely violent, relatively fearless individuals who profess and conduct themselves as if they do not care whether they live or die. They frequently attack staff as well as other prisoners. Examples of this extreme form of recalcitrance abound. George Jackson, held many years in lockup, wrote:

> This monster—the monster they've engendered in me—will return to torment its maker, from the grave, the pit, the profoundest pit. Hurl me into the next existence, the descent into hell won't turn me. I'll crawl back to dog his trail forever. They won't defeat my revenge, never, never. I'm part of a righteous people who anger slowly, but rage undammed. We'll gather at this door in such a number that the rumbling of our feet will make the earth tremble. I'm going to charge them for this twenty-eight years without gratification. I'm going to charge them like a maddened, wounded, rogue male elephant—ears flared, trunk raised, trumpet blaring. I'll do my dance in his chest, and the only thing he'll ever see in my eyes is a dagger to pierce his cruel heart. This is one nigger who is positively displeased. I'll never forgive, I'll never forget, and if I'm guilty of anything at all it's of not leaning on them enough. War without terms.[26]

Jackson, after he had succeeded in overpowering guards who had escorted him back to lockup in San Quentin and in releasing other prisoners in the unit, was shot and killed while running toward San Quentin's front gate. Some of the prisoners he had released proceeded to murder two prisoners and two guards in the lockup unit.

The two prisoners who each murdered a guard while being escorted by four guards at Marion in 1983 were fellow AB members who had been held in lockup for many years and who had vowed they would both kill a guard on that day. They murdered the guards even though they understood that they would suffer severe, immediate, and long-term consequences. They were beyond caring about consequences, or even their own lives.

In New York, Willie Bosket, who has served most of his life in prison and has been held in lockup for years, told the court which had just sentenced him to an additional 25 years to life for stabbing a prison guard:

> The sentence this court can impose on me means nothing. I laugh at you, I laugh at this court, I laugh at Mr. Prosecutor, I laugh at this entire damn system. I'll haunt this damn system. I am what the system created but never expected.[27]

Psychological Impairment. Since the introduction of our first "penitentiaries," in which prisoners were placed in complete solitary confinement, observers have concluded that isolation from others and extreme reduction of activities produces considerable psychological damage. Charles Dickens, who visited Eastern Penitentiary, the first "solitary" prison, wrote:

> I am persuaded that those who devised this system [solitary confinement] . . . do not know what it is that they are doing. . . . I hold that this slow and daily tampering with the mysteries of the brain, to be immeasurably worse than any torture of the body. . . .
>
> My firm conviction is that, independent of the mental anguish it occasions—an anguish so acute and so tremendous, that all imagination of it must fall far short of the reality—it wears the mind into a morbid state, which renders it unfit for the rough contact and busy action of the world. It is my fixed opinion that those who have undergone this punishment, must pass into society again morally unhealthy and diseased.[28]

Regrettably, only a few systematic studies of the effects of confinement in lockup situations have been conducted. In one, Richard McCleery found that prisoners held in lockup settings for long periods were very prone to developing paranoid delusion belief systems.[29] Dr. Terry A. Kupers, a psychiatrist with long experience with prisons who was assigned to give expert testimony in a suit involving California lockup units, wrote to the court:

> Certainly, patients I see in the community who have spent any length of time in Security Housing, Management Control or Adjustment Center units at San Quentin have continued to display irrational fears of violence against themselves, and have demonstrated little ability to control their own rage. I know from many psychotherapies I have conducted and histories I have taken, that even when a patient entered prison angry, the largest part of the fear and rage was bred by the prison experience itself. . . .
>
> Some of these men [prisoners held in lockup for long periods] suffer mental "breakdowns," be they schizophrenic, depressive, hysterical or other. A much larger number suffer less visible but very deep psychological scars. They do not "break down," but they remain anxious, angry, depressed, insecure or confused, and then likely cover over these feelings with superficial bravado. They might later commit suicide, or merely fail to adjust when released, and become another statistic of recidivism.[30]

Kupers summarized the psychiatric liteature on the effects of lockup in the following statement to the court:

> There is general agreement today in the scientific community that the stress of life in segregation is the larger cause of high incidence rates of mental disorders amongst prisoners.[31]

A Pelican Bay SHU prisoner puts it well:

> If you have not been informed of this new SHU program here in Pelican Bay, well, I think hell is a better place than this as it is built to break people. Since I have been here [one month] a man has gone literally nutty in the mind. What can you expect when you're isolated from all human contact? You sleep, eat, go to a yard by yourself, go to classification just to be told that you'll stay in the hole until you parole, die, or *debrief*, rat![32]

Social Impairment. It was pointed out in Chapter 3 that all prisoners confront extreme difficulties in adjusting to outside life and in achieving basic viability, and most of their problems stem from having been a prisoner. One of the reasons for this is that they have become profoundly habituated to the prison routine, which is quite different from outside patterns and have been imbued with various forms and layers of the prisoner perspective. Prisoners who have been held in lockup encounter greater difficulties because the routine in lockup is more rigid and "abnormal." In addition, many or most lockup prisoners have been influenced by the more extreme and deviant viewpoints (e.g., that of the "outlaw") that prevail in lockup and suffer extreme anxiety and paranoia about living in a world of conspiracies, threats, and actual violence.

Most persons held in lockup settings are eventually released to the outside, often directly from lockup. A SHU prisoner makes this point well:

> OK. I've been in jail now eight years. Let's say I was going home tomorrow, do you mean to tell me I sit here for eight years confined in a cell resentful of things, chained every minute of my time inside my cell. And they say I am just too dangerous for anything but tomorrow they will parole me to the streets. Is there logic there? There is no logic there. The guy is paroled from these units, straight from the cells, straight to the situation, straight to the streets. How in the hell are they suppose to function out there? Is it possible? It is not anywhere possible. There is no decompression time, there is no reorientation time or nothing. When I am paroled I will be paroled to the streets, the outside to where you're at, you know what I mean. But in the meantime every time I see you, I will be setting like this.[33]

We should be concerned by the fact that the prison systems are spewing out such damaged human material, most of whom will disappear into our social trash heap, politely labeled the "homeless" or the underclass, or, worse, will violently lash out, perhaps murdering or raping someone, and then be taken back to the dungeon.

NOTES

1. Much of the information provided in this chapter is based on the experience of the two authors. James Austin was an employee of the Illinois Department of Corrections from 1970 to 1974, and

John Irwin was an inmate in the California Department of Corrections from 1952 to 1957. Since then, both authors have been involved in many studies of prisons and jails and have served as expert witnesses for both plaintiffs and defendants in numerous court cases involving the Illinois, Florida, Texas, Nevada, New Mexico, and California prison systems and the New Orleans, Philadelphia, Seattle, San Diego, San Francisco, Chicago, and New York City jail systems.

2. In ongoing lawsuits in California (*Wright* v. *Enomoto, Toussaint* v. *McCarthy*) involving issues surrounding the use of administrative segregation, the federal court adopted the term "lockup" to designate all forms of administrative segregation except protective custody. This was because the California Department of Corrections continued to develop new "units" that they claimed were different than older ones and therefore not subject to the earlier court rulings.

3. When they first began this expansion, prison administrators usually presented the new policies as nonpunitive and planned new segregation units so they would not be as cruel as solitary confinement. In California, where segregation has been used more than in any other state, initial expansion of segregation units was justified with a therapeutic rationale. In 1956, California prison administrators requested and received funds from the state legislature to construct new housing units or convert existing units to sections called "adjustment centers," which were intended to hold prisoners who were not responding to the rehabilitative programs. According to the original plan, these prisoners would receive more intensive rehabilitative strategies, such as intensive counseling and therapy. The adjustment centers were built, but no special rehabilitative programs were introduced.

4. By 1992, at least 15,578 prisoners were locked up in administrative segregation units. This figure was obtained by adding the 13,356 listed in the Justice Department's *Corrections Yearbook* (1992) to the 2,322 that were in California "special security" units and not listed in the *Yearbook*. The California figure was obtained from Offender Information Services Branch, California Department of Corrections. Alabama and Missouri clump segregation and protective custody together and were not

included. The number in federal prison segregation units was also not available.

5. From a letter sent to the Prison Law Collective in San Francisco, California, and distributed by them in 1975 in an unpublished document titled "Descriptions of O Wing Soledad."
6. George Jackson, *Soledad Brother* (New York: Bantam Books, 1970), pp. 23, 164.
7. Ruling of Alfonso Zirpoli, Federal District Judge, Northern California District, in *Johnny L. Spain et al.* v. *Raymond K. Procunier et al.,* December 18, 1975, p. 5.
8. Interview, San Quentin prisoner, 1979.
9. See Min S. Yee, *The Melancholy History of Soledad Prison* (New York: Harper & Row, 1973) for a complete description of the events and the court decision.
10. Declaration for U.S. District Court for Northern California by Terry Kupers, M.D., *Wright* v. *Enomoto,* June 30, 1980, pp. 5, 7, 9.
11. Robert Slater, "Psychiatric Intervention in an Atmosphere of Terror," *American Journal of Forensic Psychiatry* 7, 1 (1986): 9, 8.
12. This description of Marion was taken from David A. Ward and Allen F. Breed, *The United States Penitentiary, Marion, Illinois: A Report to the Judiciary Committee, United States House of Representatives* (Washington, D.C.: U.S. Government Printing Office, October, 1984).
13. Ibid., pp. 11–12.
14. Ibid., p. 32.
15. Many guards have been seriously assaulted by prisoners locked in their cells in California adjustment centers. Several have been killed.
16. *Los Angeles Times,* May 1, 1990,
17. *Corrections Digest,* June 27, 1990, p. 9.
18. *The Sunday Oklahoma,* February 24, 1991.
19. *The New York Times,* February 20, 1991.
20. One of the authors asked a former director of the California Department of Corrections, who had worked for several years overseeing the classification process, how reliable he thought

information from informers was. He responded, "About 30 percent."

21. Interview, San Quentin, March 1983.
22. From prisoners' files read in March 1983.
23. Robert Schultz, "'Life in SHU': An Ethnographic Study of Pelican Bay State Prison," M.S. thesis, Humboldt State University, April 1991, p. 104.
24. From a letter written to the Soledad Defense Committee in 1971 and circulated in an unpublished document labeled "Descriptions of O Wing Ciliated," p. 3.
25. A frequently repeated statement by prisoners who have adopted an extremely hostile and violent-prone identity.
26. George Jackson, *Soledad Brother* (New York: Bantam Books, 1970), pp. 164–65.
27. *The New York Times,* April 20, 1989.
28. Charles Dickens, *American Notes and Pictures from Italy* (London: Oxford University Press, 1957), pp. 99, 109.
29. Terry A. Kupers, "Authoritarianism and the Belief System of Incorrigibles," in Donald R. Cressey, *The Prison* (New York: Holt, Rinehart and Winston, 1961).
30. Declaration to the U.S. District Court for the Northern District of California, *Wright* v. *Enomoto,* June 30, 1980, pp. 5, 15.
31. Declaration to the United States District Court, Northern District of California, *Wright* v. *Enomoto,* July 23, 1980, p. 4. Dr. Kupers specifically cited the following articles in reaching his conclusions: W. Bromber et al., "The Relation of Psychosis, Mental Defect, and Personality Types to Crime," *Journal of Criminal Law and Criminology* 28 (1973): 70–89; S. B. Guze et al., "Criminality and Psychiatric Disorders," *Archives of General Psychiatry* 20 (1969): 583–91; J. Kloech, "Schizophrenia and Delinquency," in *The Mentally Abnormal Offender* (1968): 19–28; D. Wiersman, "Crime and Schizophrenics," *Excerpta Criminologica* 6 (1966): 169–81.
32. Letter from Pelican Bay prisoner sent to Prisoners' Rights Union, Sacramento, California.
33. Schultz, "Life in SHU," p. 153.

5

Release

Eventually, the vast majority of prisoners leave prison. In 1991, nearly 420,000 inmates were released from prison, the majority of these (nearly 340,000) to some form of parole or probation supervision (Table 5-1).[1] Of the prisoners released to parole, about half are released at the discretion of the state's parole board; the remaining parole releases occur after the inmate has completed his or her mandatory period of confinement less good time credits awarded and/or earned by the inmate. A growing number of inmates, however, are released with no supervision whatsoever as some states abolish parole supervision or become increasingly reluctant to parole inmates.

In this chapter we examine what happens to inmates who are released after having spent several years in confinement and the obstacles they face in trying to make it on the streets without reverting to criminal behavior.

TIME IN PRISON AND ON PAROLE

According to the U.S. Department of Justice, the length of stay (LOS) for first releases from prison in 1989 averages 22 months, with a median LOS of only 13 months (Table 5-2).[2] Although these two statistics might sound like a relatively short period of incarceration,

TABLE 5-1 Prison Releases—1991

	Number	Percent
Total releases	419,783	100.0
Conditional releases	339,439	80.9
Parole releases	159,731	38.1
Supervised mandatory releases	116,857	27.8
Probation releases	21,014	5.0
Other conditional releases	41,837	10.0
Unconditional releases	55,288	13.2
Expiration of sentence	51,288	12.2
Commutation of sentence	385	0.1
Other Releases	26,056	6.0

Source: U.S. Department of Justice, Bureau of Justice Statistics, *Correction Populations in the United States, 1990* (Washington, D.C.: U.S. Government Printing Office, 1992), table 5.13.

the average length of time in prison has been increasing as prison sentences became longer during the past decade. These statistics are grossly misleading because they greatly *underestimate* the total length of incarceration for most offenders for several reasons.

One reason is that the 22-month LOS figure only refers to persons who are making their first release to parole on their current sentence. These first releases are prisoners who are released to parole or probation after reaching what is referred to as their initial minimum release date. If this minimum release date is the inmate's initial parole release date, then the parole board must agree to grant a parole.[3]

Consequently, this category of releases excludes the large number of inmates who have returned to prison for parole violations and who spent many additional months in confinement before being rereleased to parole or being discharged after completing their entire sentence (i.e., "maxing out"). As we will show later, many inmates are returned to prison as technical violators, thus adding to their original period of confinement for the same sentence. In California and Nevada, for example, parolees who are revoked for technical reasons spend an average of seven to eight months in prison before being reinstated on parole or "maxing out" on their original sentence.[4]

TABLE 5-2 Prison Releases and Time Served in Prison for Selected States*

	Number	Percent
Total prison releases	298,353	100.0
First release on sentence	215,963	72.4
Violators rereleased	82,390	27.6
Method of release		
Parole board decision	103,678	35.7
Mandatory parole	96,077	33.9
Expiration of sentence	56,691	15.0
Escape/AWOL	6,169	2.3
Death	1,462	0.5
Other releases	16,843	6.1
Unknown reason for release	17,433	6.5
Time served in prison—first releases		
State prison	22 months	
Federal prison	29 months	
Median education at release	Tenth grade	
Median age	29 years	

* Based on information provided by 36 states and the Federal Bureau of Prisons as reported by the Bureau of Justice Statistics, *National Corrections Reporting Program, 1989,* pp. 21–30.

The same California data show that over 36,000 parolees, who had spent an average of 5–7 months in custody, were revoked in 1991. Given that such a large proportion of inmates are experiencing parole revocations, the total period of confinement for most inmates, taking into account parole revocations, is certainly 2–3 months higher than reported by the U.S. Department of Justice. Omission of these data from the overall length of stay calculation can be significant depending upon the state's use of parole revocations.

Second, the 22-month figure ignores the fact that most inmates spend many months in jail in pretrial status awaiting their sentence. Illinois inmates spend an average of seven to eight months waiting in county jails before they are transferred to state prisons. In California, the average amount of time spent in jail is five months.[5] Adding these periods of pretrial imprisonment increases the national average to about 27 to 28 months.

Third, the current cohort of prison releases does not accurately reflect recent changes in sentencing laws that require greater numbers of inmates to serve extremely long periods of time. For example, in Florida, offenders who are "habitualized" since 1987 must serve an average of eight years before being eligible for release. These inmates' lengths of stay will not begin to appear until 1995. The current LOS for Florida inmates based on 1992 releases was only 1.75 years. However, if the projected LOS for the habitual inmates (and others serving very long sentences) is incorporated, the actual LOS is over three years.[6]

Those inmates released to parole or probation must spend the remainder of their original sentence either on parole or on some prescribed period of supervision (e.g., 12 months, 24 months, etc.). The average period of parole supervision is approximately 23 months, which means that most inmates will spend about four years (two years in prison and jail, and two more years on parole supervision) before they have completed their sentence (Figure 5-1).

Rates of Rearrest After Release. During this period of supervision, many released inmates experience tremendous difficulties in adjusting to the outside world without being rearrested and returning to prison and jail. In general, most inmates are rearrested at least once after being released from prison. The U.S. Department of Justice conducted a followup study of 108,580 inmates released from prison to parole in 11 states in 1983 and found that 63 percent were rearrested at least once for a felony or a serious misdemeanor within three years. However, the vast majority (85 percent) were for property, drugs, and public disorder crimes.[7] Studies by Rand and the National Council on Crime and Delinquency (NCCD) of inmates released from Illinois and California prisons demonstrated that about 40 to 45 percent were rearrested within the first year, whereas 60 to 70 percent had been rearrested for felonies and serious misdemeanors within three years.[8]

These high arrest rates have led many to argue that more and not less imprisonment is needed to reduce crime. Yet findings from several studies suggest that imprisonment, as compared to other penal dispositions, does not reduce convicted offenders' involvement in crime.

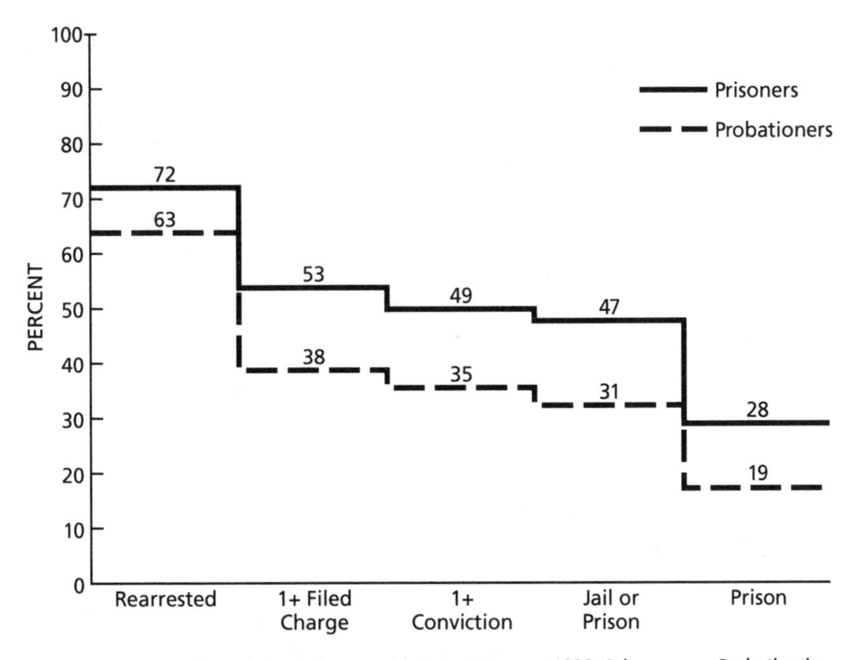

Source: Joan Petersilia and Susan Turner, with Joyce Peterson. 1986. *Prison versus Probation in California. Implications For Crime and Offender Recedivism* Santa Monica, CA: The Rand Corporation

FIGURE 5-1 Recidivism among Probationers and Matched Prisoners: Total Sample Combined

The often neglected study by the Rand Corporation, sponsored by the U.S. Department of Justice, compared the two-year rearrest rates of a group of felons sent to California prisons with a group who were matched on crime seriousness, past record, and other relevant characteristics but were granted probation instead of prison. The results revealed that the persons sentenced to prison were rearrested, reconvicted, and resentenced to jail or prison at significantly higher rates than the persons who were sentenced to probation (Table 5-3).[9]

Even though prison has apparently increased the likelihood that they will commit future crimes, ex-prisoners are still less likely to commit crime than they were before being sent to prison. In other words, their rate of rearrest is declining compared to the rate that existed before they were sentenced to prison. Two studies of released felons in California and Illinois conducted by the NCCD showed that

TABLE 5-3 Parole Releases and Time Served on Parole for Selected States*

	Number	Percent
Total parole releases	155,346	100.0
Method of release		
Successful	60,145	38.7
Absconded	873	0.6
Returned to jail or prison	91,145	58.7
Death	419	0.3
Other	2,764	1.8
Time served on parole		
State inmates—successful discharges	23 months	
Federal inmates	53 months	
Median education at release from parole	10th grade	
Median age at release from parole	29 years	

* Based on information provided by 27 states and the Federal Bureau of Prisons by the U.S. Department of Justice, Bureau of Justice Statistics, *National Corrections Reporting Program, 1989* (Washington, D.C.: U.S. Government Printing Office, 1992), pp. 37–50.

the arrest rates of released prisoners were about half of the rate prior to imprisonment. The California study found that the number of arrests for prisoners released to the streets over two years dropped by over 50 percent compared to the number that occurred two years before the inmates were sentenced to prison and that the severity of the crimes also declined by 50 percent during the two-year followup period.[10]

The Illinois study also found a 64 percent decline in the rate of arrest 12 months after release from prison as compared to the 12 months prior to imprisonment (.80 arrests per year per released inmate versus 2.20 arrests per year prior to prison).[11] The NCCD study also showed that significant proportions of these arrests are for minor property or drug use crimes that do not result in a conviction or resentencing to prison. Instead, the high arrest rates often reflect traditional police practices of "rounding up the usual suspects." The NCCD studies also demonstrated that although prison releases are frequently rearrested, their overall impact on crime rates in the two states is about 2 percent or less.

The reductions in arrest rates for released inmates is largely the result of maturation effects: as inmates get older, they burn out and are unable to maintain their previous criminal lifestyles. The highest crime rates are for males between the ages of 15 and 24, whereas the average age for released prisoners is over 30, well beyond their most productive crime-producing years. This, in part, explains the limits of incarceration as a workable crime-reducing strategy. The ranks of released prisoners are replaced by the next generation of lower-class prison-bound males nurtured in inner-city communities riddled with poverty, drug abuse, and violence.

THE RISING TIDE OF PAROLE FAILURES

Although an arrest does not necessarily result in a conviction or a new sentence for the recently released inmate, an arrest or even behavior that is noncriminal can result in an inmate's return to prison for many months. Earlier studies indicated that less than 25 percent of all parolees were returned to prison for new crimes or technical violations over a three-year followup period and that most of these arrests were for property and drug offenses. In fact, the Justice Department estimated at that time that only 29 to 42 percent of all prison releases will be returned to prison *in their lifetimes* (BJS, 1985).[12]

Those earlier trends have changed considerably, however. Today most inmates do not get off of parole without some further legal difficulties. Since 1980, the number of parole violations has increased nationally from 28,817 to 122,156 in 1989, representing a 324 percent increase. Table 5-4 summarizes data from 27 states and the Federal Bureau of Prisons, as reported by the U.S. Department of Justice, tracking the reason why inmates are released from parole supervision. Only 39 percent of all persons discharged off parole in 1989 were classified as "successful" discharges. Nearly 60 percent were returned to prison or jail for one of two reasons: (1) they had committed new crimes while under parole supervision and were resentenced to prison, or (2) they had failed to comply with the conditions of parole supervision as determined by the parole board authorities.

This trend is attributable in large part to dramatic changes in the nature of parole supervision and the imposition of increasingly more severe conditions of supervision on parolees. Instead of a system designed to help prisoners readjust to a rapidly changing and more competitive economic system, the current parole system has been designed to catch and punish inmates for petty and nuisance-type behaviors that do not in themselves draw a prison term.

Technical violations are by far the more frequent form of parole failure than being resentenced for a new crime, which occurs at a far lower rate. Technical violations represent a wide array of noncriminal behaviors (see Table 5-4). For example, an inmate may have failed to appear for scheduled office visits with the parole agent, failed to attend counseling sessions, failed to notify the parole agent of a change of address, or failed to maintain "gainful" employment. Technical violations can also include subsequent arrests without convictions or failure to pass drug tests—suggesting continued drug use—or may simply reflect unsubstantiated suspicions by parole authorities.

Unlike the criminal courts, parole revocation hearings do not require the same level of proof to trigger a return to prison. Although the Morissey decision by the U.S. Supreme Court grants parolees the right to a partial "due process" hearing, they still are not afforded such basic rights at these hearings as the right to counsel or the right to call witnesses, an impartial judge and jury, or most of the features of a *full* due process proceeding. More important, a parolee's parole status can be revoked if the board feels there is a preponderance of evidence that the parolee was not meeting parole obligations. This means that parolees who are arrested but not found guilty can have their parole status revoked, be returned to prison, and remain in prison until their original sentence expires.

Some parole board officials view these broad discretionary powers over parolees as a positive feature of parole, since it allows them to reimprison prisoners with greater speed and certainty than if the charges had been brought before the criminal courts. For example, revoking parole status and reincarcerating the prisoner is accomplished without involving the district attorney, public defender, law enforcement official, or judge. Parole revocation hearings often are pro forma ceremonies lasting less than five minutes before a parole board hearing officer, whose recommendation is forwarded to the full board for approval.

TABLE 5-4 Selected Conditions of Parole in Effect in Fifty-one Jurisdictions, 1988

Condition of Parole	Number of Jurisdictions	Percent
Obey all federal, state, and local laws	50	98.0
Report to the parole officer as directed and answer all reasonable inquiries by the parole officer	49	96.1
Refrain from possessing a firearm or other dangerous weapon unless granted written permission	47	92.2
Remain within the jurisdiction of the court and notify the parole officer of any change in residence	46	90.2
Permit the parole officer to visit the parolee at home or elsewhere	42	82.4
Obey all rules and regulations of the parole supervision agency	40	78.4
Maintain gainful employment	40	78.4
Abstain from association with persons with criminal records	31	60.8
Pay all court-ordered fines, restitution, or other financial penalties	27	52.9
Meet family responsibilities and support dependents	24	47.1
Undergo medical or psychiatric treatment and/or enter and remain in a specified institution, if so ordered by the court	23	45.1
Pay supervision fees	19	37.3
Attend a prescribed secular course of study or vocational training	9	17.6
Perform community service	7	13.7

Source: Edward E. Rhine, William R. Smith, and Donald W. Jackson, *Paroling Authorities Recent History and Current Practice* (Laurel, Md.: American Correctional Association, 1991).

A recent study by NCCD for the Nevada legislature found that over 1,000 of the 6,200 inmate population were either parole or probation technical violators.[13] A closer analysis of the behaviors surrounding these technical violations discovered that the vast majority were for behaviors such as failing to maintain steady employment, failure to participate in drug treatment, failure to report changes in address, and arrests for misdemeanor or traffic violations. Some typical examples of the type of behaviors that triggered a parole violation in Nevada are as follows:

> Case #1: This offender was originally received out of Clark County on 3/9/92, to serve a 3 year term for Attempt Under the Influence of a Controlled Substance. He was paroled on 10/1/92, and returned to prison as a parole violator on 3/19/93. His parole was revoked to expiration for general rule violations (failure to maintain verifiable residence, failure to pay supervision fees). He will discharge from prison on 1/10/94; when he discharges he will have served 9 months in prison for his violation of parole.
>
> Case #2: This prisoner was originally received on 2/22/90, from Clark County serving a 5 year term for Burglary. This subject paroled on 10/30/91, and returned as a parole violator on 10/8/92. This subject's parole was violated for failure to maintain verifiable residence and employment, reports, failure to participate in drug testing and out-patient substance abuse counseling and violating the house arrest program. He is scheduled to discharge this prison term on 5/24/93. This subject will serve over 7 months in prison for violating these technical parole rules.
>
> Case #3: She was originally received on 9/5/86, from Clark County serving a 5 year sentence for Attempt Possession of a Cheating Device with a consecutive 1 year sentence of Attempt Under Influence of a Controlled Substance. She was paroled on 3/25/88, and returned as a violator on 9/15/88 after being arrested by her parole officer for rules involving residence, employment, reports, and failure to attend outpatient substance abuse counseling. At the time of the arrest she was being treated for pneumonia at Washoe Medical Center which was related to her deteriorating health problems from HIV infection. Her parole status was revoked and she was eventually released on 4/4/89. This subject was completely incapacitated at the time of

discharge and released to her parents. She died several days after discharge and the medical bills accumulated by the Department of Prisons totaled $21,026.90.

OBSTACLES TO MAKING IT AFTER RELEASE

Why is it that so many prisoners have such a difficult time making it on parole? Given their social and economic situation, one might better ask: Why do so many actually make it? Their transition to the outside world is replete with hurdles, pitfalls, and traps that make it extremely difficult for all and defeat many. These obstacles range from finding a job and staying off drugs to dealing with the parole agent. To probe the dimensions of this problem, we interviewed 14 parolees in April 1993. Their case studies illustrate some typical difficulties.[14]

The Shock of "Reentry". Most ex-inmates pass suddenly from a highly routinized, controlled, reduced, and slow-paced prison life into the complex, fast-moving, impersonal world of the "streets." Because they are assimilated into prison routine and culture, the transition usually disorganizes, disturbs, and depresses them—especially those inmates who have spent many years incarcerated. Just imagine the problems that highly skilled and well-educated white males would have in getting a job, buying a car, and finding a place to live after two years of imprisonment. For the uneducated and unemployable who must face a rapidly changing and increasingly competitive and unforgiving society, the odds are almost insurmountable.

> The cars, buses, people, buildings, roads, stores, lights, noises, and animals are things [they haven't] experienced at first hand for quite some time. The most ordinary transactions of the civilian have dropped from [their] repertoire of automatic maneuvers. Getting on a streetcar, ordering something at a hot dog stand, entering a theater are strange. Talking to people whose accent, style of speech, gestures, and vocabulary are slightly different is difficult. The entire stimulus world—the sights, sounds, and smells—is strange.[15]

Beyond overcoming the initial shock of "reentry," released prisoners must struggle to achieve some minimal level of economic viability. To do this in a conventional fashion, they must immediately locate some form of affordable housing, gather sufficient clothing and other basic accoutrements—tools, and toiletries—and get a job. They have scant resources for accomplishing these meager goals. State prison systems usually provide a small amount of money, $200 or so, and a few provide transitional institutional supports—such as halfway houses or arrangements with social welfare agencies. These supports, however, are temporary and merely prolong the eventual problem of trying to make it without going back to prison.

Some prisoners have saved a little, even several hundred dollars, from money earned in prison "pay" jobs, which usually pay considerably less than $1 an hour. A minority have help from their families. However, most must make it on their own resources and capabilities, which are typically limited and damaged. As we pointed out in Chapter 2, most prisoners enter prison poorly educated and vocationally unskilled, with limited work experience. And prison has done little to improve their preparation for the outside work world; in fact, it has often worsened it. As we pointed out earlier, prisoners seldom receive any appropriate job training, and the habits they learn in prison are inconsistent with outside work routines.

Finding a Job. Despite research showing that providing employment or other forms of economic assistance significantly reduces the likelihood of recidivism, most prison systems are unable or unwilling to assist inmates.[16] Released inmates confront sizeable barriers to getting even the most demeaning forms of employment because they are stigmatized as ex-convicts. Most employers will not hire ex-convicts and so, when applying for a job, the "ex" must either tell the employer that he has a record and likely be denied employment or lie and take the chance that the employer will not run a record check or that a parole agent will not inform the employer. Also, many jobs require bonding, special licenses, or union membership, all of which are unavailable to most ex-convicts.

The ex-convict stands at the very end of society's growing line of job seekers. At the end of the 1960s, when the country had more employment opportunities for blue-collar workers than it does presently, there was some movement to reduce the employment barriers for ex-convicts when studies revealed an employment rate of around 50 percent (which seemed dismal at the time). At present, this rate is much lower. In California in 1991, only 21 percent of the state's parolees had full-time jobs. Seventy percent were not employed, and an additional 9 percent had "casual" employment.[17] The following two cases reveal the difficulties released prisoners have in trying to locate a job.

> *R. C., a 22-year-old black man.* I've been looking for work for two weeks. I'm living with friends, cause my mother can't help me. I've been staying away from my old neighborhood and friends, cause I don't want to get back into that life. I've been pretty nervous cause I don't know how to live like this. If I was going back to selling drugs, I wouldn't be nervous, cause I would know what I was gonna do. But I made up my mind I wasn't gonna sell no drugs.
>
> I go to different places, fill out applications. I've been to San Leandro, Hayward, Oakland, Berkeley. I'm in the process of getting my California ID. I have to have that. Now every day I am going to different places and trying to get a job. I got a friend who got a job at the Oakland Airport. He says something might come up there. If I don't get a job through some agency or friends, I'm gonna do something I thought I would never do—work for McDonalds.

> *K. B., a 38-year-old black man.* I been meeting R.C. [above] and we been going up and down the streets applying everywhere. Wherever I tell him to meet me, he is there on time. I was supposed to get this light industrial job. They kept putting obstacles in front of me and I talked my way over them every time, till she brought up my being on parole and then she went sour on me. If they catch me lying on the job application about being in prison or being on parole, they will violate me and give me four months.
>
> I was over to Hertz, applying for a job detailing cars. They pay $9 a hour. They told me they would give me a job if I had a driver's license. I gotta have $50 to get my license reissued. $35 for a ticket and $15 for the fee. The agent doesn't have a fund to loan me any. They used to have a fund, but the parolees didn't pay the money back. If I could get my license, I could work for Avis or Hertz.

> I had dry-cleaning training a long time ago, but this time I wasn't in long enough to go through the program. It takes several years. You have to have the paper to get a job. I could jump in and clean anything—silks, wools, remove any spot, use all the chemicals, but I don't got any paper. They won't let you start without the paper. And they don't have any programs where they are giving you the old training and certifying you.

Trail 'em, Nail 'em, Jail 'em. Being on parole means being under the supervision of parole agents, who have peace officer status. Parole officers are equipped with extraordinary police powers: they can enforce a set of "conditions of parole," which are much more restrictive than penal statutes, and they are not restrained by constitutional protections against invasion of privacy and illegal search and seizure. Parole agents can enter a parolee's residence at any time in the day or night, search the parolee at the agent's discretion, or place the parolee in jail any time they desire and charge the parolee with violation of parole, either for new crimes or for violation of the conditions of parole.

> I go to the parole agent and tell him I want to get a job. "Uh, come back and see me next week." I mean, it's not really his fault because he got three hundred other guys. And he doesn't even know me. All he knows is my number is three seven such and such. All he knows—if he wants to keep his job, all he got to do is have me come in once a week, piss in the bottle. As long as the bottle don't show no drugs in it, I can stay on the street another week. First time the piss is not good, all he gotta do is send me to jail, that's it. He put my file over there in "inactive," and that's it. He's still got his job, he goes on—you know, they don't have to get personally involved with you. 'Cause they can't. You got three hundred guys—how you get involved with three hundred guys?[18]

Commensurate with the toughening of sentencing laws and the demise of the rehabilitation model, parole supervision has been transformed ideologically from a social service to a law enforcement system. During the rehabilitative era (the 1950s and 1960s), most states sought to combine policing and rehabilitative services in their parole administration. Parole agents were viewed as paternalistic figures who mixed authority and help. The punitive swing in corrections and the fiscal crisis experienced by most states has transformed parole more and more into a policing operation. Instead of developing individualized plans to help the prisoners locate a job, find a residence, or locate needed drug treatment services, the new parole system is bent on surveillance and detection. Parolees are routinely and randomly checked for illegal drug use, failure to locate or maintain a job, moving without permission, or any other number of petty and nuisance-type behaviors that don't conform to the rules of parole.

On detection of any of these acts or on the parolee's arrest for any crime, the parole officer holds the option of having the parolee arrested and placed in the local jail until the parole board can review the charges. In many states, parolees can wait weeks in the local jail until a representative from the parole board makes a determination on whether the behavior is sufficiently serious to warrant revocation and return to prison.

A parolee we interviewed ended up on general assistance, abusing drugs, and finally in a drug program after he lost a good job because of his agent's enforcement of the rules:

> *D. H., a 51-year-old white man.* I looked for a place to stay in San Francisco, so I moved in with a friend across the bay in Hayward. I got a job as a bank courier. I wasn't carrying any money and it was a good job. My agent told me to quit it and move back to the city. I hadn't been able to find a job in the city, so I told him, "Would you rather have me back on G.A. and selling dope?" He said he couldn't tell me to do that.

Drug Testing. As the system has been reoriented toward a law enforcement system, the methods of surveillance have been strengthened. The most powerful tool for the new parole agent is the urine analysis test. Nowhere is this tactic used more forcibly than in California, where almost all released inmates are subject to weekly urine analysis tests. The first thing a parolee is instructed to do on arrival at the parole officer's office is to urinate in a bottle and have a chemical test completed. Since most of these inmates have rather extensive histories of drug use, it is predictable that many will occasionally fail the drug test and subsequently have their paroles revoked.

Because of the widespread use of drug testing, California, until this past year, has led the country in parole violations.[19] Prior to 1993, two out of every five parole violations that occurred nationally in 1988 occurred in California. Over 65 percent of all California parolees were returned to prison within two years, and over half of all prison admissions were parole violators. Of those who were returned to prison for parole violation, approximately 80 percent were returned without a conviction for a new felony prison term. Most were re-arrested for nonviolent misdemeanor crimes. Of those rearrested, 30 percent were not convicted, but the board ordered that these parolees spend another four to five months in prison—at a cost of over $7,000 per prisoner. By way of comparison, offenders sentenced to local jails for these crimes spent only 43 days in custody.[20]

Intensive Supervision Programs. Intensive supervision programs (ISP) also place additional obstacles in the path of parolees and result in more parole failures. Hailed by criminologists as the new wave of "intermediate sanctions," these programs were first created by the courts to divert offenders who otherwise would have been imprisoned had the program not existed. However, they have also been used by parole agencies to escalate levels of supervision for offenders paroled from prison. ISPs for the "back end" of the correctional system are intended to encourage parole boards to release offenders who pose a somewhat higher risk to public safety and would not have been released had the ISP not existed. By releasing these marginal cases on ISP, the inmate's expected length of stay in prison can be shortened, thus reducing the prison population. For both probationers and parolees, specialized treatment programs were also to be part of the ISP regimen, although this rarely has been the case. The overall expectation was that these programs would also reduce these offenders' recidivism rates and therefore be more cost effective as compared to traditional forms of incarceration.

Evaluations of these programs have shown just the opposite results. A number of experimental studies by the Rand Corporation have found that persons placed in these programs violate parole for technical reasons at a far greater rate than those receiving regular supervision, even though their rearrest rates were essentially equal.[21] These programs also tend to be far more expensive than regular supervision and have had little if any impact on prison crowding. Because of the highly restrictive nature of the program's eligibility criteria, these programs are quite small in size (50 to 150 offenders diverted or released on parole each year) and often cease to exist once federal funds used to start the programs dry up.

The higher technical violation failure rates for ISP cases is simply the result of programs that provide more supervision but not many more services. Consequently, parole and probation officers are able to detect more petty behavior than before. But more important, the parole officer is able to use this information against the inmate to justify revocation and recommitment to prison.

Electronic Monitoring. Many ISP programs are also adding electronic monitoring technology to their monitoring capabilities. The last national estimate indicated that over 12,000 offenders were under electronic monitoring on any given day.[22] The U.S. Department of Justice reported that in 1989 over 5,000 probationers and parolees were being supervised via electronic monitoring.[23] In Illinois, over 200 newly released inmates are under a house arrest status with electronic monitoring. In such a situation, the inmate cannot leave his residence without calling his parole officer to do such normal things as purchasing groceries, picking up the mail, or running any number of regular errands associated with modern life.

As with the ISP evaluations, rigorous studies of electronic monitoring programs have found neither negative nor positive results relating to rearrest.[24] Offenders admitted to such programs respond the same as or worse than offenders placed under normal supervision. In fact, the NCCD study of the Oklahoma electronic monitoring program found that released inmates placed on electronic monitoring did worse, as a greater proportion were returned to prison for not abiding by the strict house arrest rules imposed by the electronic monitoring program.

THOSE THAT MAKE IT

Most prisoners we interviewed in our three-state study aspired to a relatively modest, stable, conventional life after prison. "I want a nice job, paying pretty good. Something to keep me busy instead of running the streets." "When I get out I want to have my kids with me, have a good job so I can support them." "I'm going to try to get into electronics. I want a job I won't get laid off on."[25] However, their chances of achieving these modest goals are slim. As already suggested, released prisoners are socially and economically damaged goods. Parolees are certainly no better equipped to make it in society after imprisonment than when they were admitted. They remain largely uneducated,[26] unskilled, and without the necessary family support system to help them make a law-abiding transition from prison to the community.

Despite these obstacles, most released prisoners eventually quit or scale down their criminal activities to a level that avoids arrest, or at least arrest for serious crimes. Since so many continue to have extreme difficulty finding and holding jobs, how, then, do they get by? What kind of life do they live?

Doing Good. A few "do all right," that is, achieve more or less permanent viability in a relatively conventional manner. They usually do so only because of the random chance of securing a good job and a niche in some conventional social world by virtue of their own individual efforts to "straighten up," often with the assistance of their family, friends, or prisoner assistance organizations. But even members of this group are likely to face periodic obstacles in being accepted as full citizens. In applying for a job from which they are not excluded by virtue of their prior criminal record, they must publicly admit their ex-convict status. When crimes are committed in their neighborhoods, they are often arrested simply because they are known to the police. Their friendships and memories are forever tied to their past prison experiences. They will always be treated by others with suspicion, fear, and distrust.

A very few—usually persons with better preparation when they leave prison, significant support from friends, family, or some program, and some luck—realize some of their higher aspirations. A 29-year-old white male who had a drug and alcohol problem since he was 15 and served two years for vehicular manslaughter was about to graduate from San Francisco State with a 3.7 grade point average and was applying for graduate school when we interviewed him. His progress demonstrates the difficulty experienced by persons who do make it.

I had about $1,200 when I got out that I had saved when I was out on OR [release on Own Recognizance program]. I knew from my crime and record I was gonna get time, so I worked and saved my money.

I first got a hotel room in downtown Burlingame, the only flea bag hotel there, and went to an AA meeting that night. The next day I went to see my parole officer and he started right off reading all my arrests, saying you did this and that. But I finally struck a deal with him that if I didn't drink or drive a car without a license he would keep off my back. But if I did, he would violate me and charge me with everything he could. He lived up to the bargain for a year and then I got another parole agent.

By then I was already in San Francisco State. I had signed up with the Rebound Project [a program that helps ex-prisoners enter San Francisco State University] while I was in CMC [a state prison near San Luis Obispo]. I had a small apartment in San Carlos for $400 a month. I was busing it to school three days a week. Two hours there and two hours back. I got a job at Walgreen's. I was selling liquor at night to guys who were just like me. But I was attending AA and had made up my mind that I was gonna change my life. And I never took a drink. Then I worked for a while selling cars. Then selling TVs at Mathews in Daly City. I bought an old beat-up Buick that had a pretty good motor and got two years out of it. About 25,000 miles.

The next parole agent was a real tough guy. First thing he told me was, "It's obvious you've been pulling some scam for a year." So he put me back on maximum custody. The other agent, even though he put on the tough guy act, he left me alone. This guy had me coming in once a week, had me pissing in the bottle, and he would show up at my house at six in the morning trying to catch me at something. But I had decided that if they were going to send me back, they were gonna have to fabricate something. I wasn't doing nothing. I didn't even have kitchen knives in my house. I made the decision, also, that I was gonna stay out of their face. I learned that in prison. If you stayed out of people's faces and stayed away from places where shit started, you wouldn't have any trouble. I never went in the day room or to the iron pile [the weight workout area]. That's where guys got stuck. So I did the same on the outside. I had to learn to keep out of people's faces outside, too. One time some guy in the library got in my face and I got back in his. I didn't have the little stamp on my ID card that you had to have to check out reference books and he wouldn't give me a book. They hadn't sent me the stamp yet. So we got into it. But I try now to keep out of everyone's face. Sometimes some of these P.C. [politically correct] students get on my nerves. The little assholes don't know shit and they're telling me what's politically correct. But I still stay out of their face.

Then I got another agent. They didn't tell me and I went to the office and the old agent said he had sent me a letter telling me that I had been transferred to a new agent. He didn't send me no letter. It's lucky I had gone to see the old agent when I did, because I was suppose to report to the new agent the next day and I wouldn't have known it and they could have violated me. This guy was an asshole too, but then I got another agent and he was like the first one. By that time I had finished two years of college and had no arrests. So he left me alone. Now, I am gonna graduate with a 3.7.

But I had a lot of luck, too. A lot of times I got behind in my rent, but I had good landlords. Really nice guys and they let me slide. They could have kicked me out and where would I have been? The parole agency wasn't gonna help me. They're too busy trying to bust guys.

Dependency. Many ex-prisoners refrain from further law violations but remain completely dependent on their families or social welfare. This is true for the following three parolees we interviewed.

K. W., a 30-year-old black man. I got out on Friday a year ago, and I got high right away. When I went to the parole agent on Monday, he asked me if I had been using and I told him I had. He said he liked my honesty, but he sent me right then to a 90-day detox at San Quentin. I didn't use no more. I been staying at home with my mother. She is just happy I'm clean. I haven't been able to find no job, but she thinks that's all right, just so I'm clean. You see, I got a younger brother and sister and an older sister, all on crack. I help them a little and protect the house. My mother is just glad I do that. She is proud of me. Shows me to her friends, says see how good he looks. I go to meetings and just stay home. I got a lady and a seven-year-old daughter, too, who I see a lot.

I'm on GA [general assistance welfare] and get $340 a month. I couldn't live on that. It's lucky I got my mother. I got phlebitis in my leg and have to take medicine. It hurts when I stand or walk too much. But I'm still gonna take a job if I get one. I want the extra spending money. But I'm not goin back on drugs. If I did, I'd just be back into buying some drugs, flipping them or burglarizing houses and factories like before.

L. F., a 48-year-old white man. I get $620 a month through SSI. I got a room on Sixth Street [skid row area] through Tenderloin Housing. It costs me $260 a month. I eat breakfasts at one of the restaurants around the hotel. For two fifty I get eggs, bacon, and potatoes. Sometimes I eat at Glide for lunch, sometimes dinner, too. Once in a while I treat myself to steak dinner.

I don't use drugs or alcohol. I mostly stay to myself, watch TV in the room. It's safer that way. Sometimes, I walk to Golden Gate Park. And I go to a movie once in a while. I can't read very much because I'm too nervous. I have a hyperactive thyroid. They found out I had it in prison. I kept losing weight. I went from around 190 to 130. The doctors there didn't know what it was and wouldn't give me any time. So I swallowed glass and told them I had. They sent me to the General Hospital and when I got there, I told them why I had done it. So they gave me all kinds of tests and found out I had the hyperactive thyroid. So I'm waiting to get some drugs for it. I've been on the list for seven months. I have an appointment in May.

I'm not goin back to prison. I can't live there. I don't know how they can treat a person like that. Least they could do is have some kind of program. There is no rehabilitation. They just shove you out the door with no support. It's scary as hell.

What I want is a job. Any job. I don't give a fuck what it is. I'll clean shitters, or whatever. At least it is something to fill my time and make me feel better about myself, something constructive.

D. R., a 51-year-old Chicano. I used drugs, speed, the first day. It scared the hell out of me. I've been clean ever since, since July, nine months. It's the first time I've been clean when I was out since I first went to the joint in the '60s. I feel kinda weird. I'm gonna stay clean and get off this parole. It's hard to do, but I'm not goin back.

I tried to get work, but there is this thing, you have to say you were in prison. If you don't, it's a violation. Who's gonna hire a 51-year-old that's been in prison most of his life?

I'm getting GA. My room's $270. That leaves me 70 bucks. Not much. I'm trying to get SSI, drugs and having been in the system all these years. They tell me that you go once and they deny you. You go again and they deny you. Then the third time they give it to you.

I eat in restaurants once in a while. But usually I buy food at the food bank. A friend of my has a hot plate. Sometimes I eat at Glide or that gay Church on Gough. I go there on Christmas, New Year, and Easter. I go up to the firehouse on Third St. where they collect toys for kids. They give out soup in the afternoon. My sister sent me some clothes and every month I buy something, like these jeans.

Most of the time I stay alone. I stay away from the TL [Tenderloin district, where there is a lot of drug dealing, prostitution, and crime]. I watch TV a lot. I go to the library and walk around a lot. I like to go to Golden Gate Park and the wharf. Last month I went back to Arkansas and visited my sister. The parole agent let me go. When I got back, he said he won a bet on me. The supervisor said I would never come back.

I go to the shelters sometimes to talk to people. I try to tell the youngsters how it is. Maybe I can help them a little, so they can stay away from the shit I got into.

Drift. Other parolees, even though their intentions before release and at the time we interviewed them were to avoid going back to prison, cross back and forth—outside and inside the law and the parole rules. For a while they hold menial jobs or live with their families, in halfway houses, or on welfare. Then they slip, start using drugs, lose their job, begin selling drugs or stealing. Usually they are arrested or "violated" by their agent and sent back, often for short periods, perhaps a 30-day detox, which in California can be done with no formal proceedings. Then they begin again to attempt to live within the law and parole rules. Two parolees we interviewed had been drifting for more than a year.

A. R., a 30-year-old black man. When I got out I moved in with my cousin in the Haight [the Haight-Ashbury district]. I wanted to stay away from the crime element, the prey-type environment. I met this guy at a club who said he thought I would be a good bouncer because I was big so I worked at this place at Turk and Eddy [in the Tenderloin district] for 10 months. I lost that job because I was staying up so late and I started using some drugs. So then I started selling a little dope. I'd take $100 and buy some crack and make $300. But I was using and the agent sent me back to San Quentin for a 90-day violation.

Then I got out and started scuffling to get by. I was cleaning the streets. A friend had a pickup and we'd go around and pick up anything. An old stove or refrigerator, sitting on the sidewalk. We picked up this old dirty Persian rug and we cleaned it up and sold it to some hippie. We were living from day to day. Then I got to using crack again and was busted in a car with a white guy, scoring. I got sent back for six months that time.

Now I'm out, no job and I don't want to go back, I'm not going back. My aspiration is to be a public relations man, but I haven't had any luck in finding anything like that.

R. R., a 30-year-old black man. I stopped in Oakland on the way home and went to MacArthur and Telegraph, saw a couple of friends and got high. I got a room in a little hotel there. After a few days I went to see my agent in San Francisco and told him I was high and needed some help. He put me in a detox program for 72 hours and then put me in Milestone. It's a halfway house for parolees. I stayed there for four months. I had a job in temporary service and had a bank account, $300. On a Friday I wanted to get high. I went back to Milestone, got my clothes, and went to the Tenderloin. I got busted on Turk St. I had just bought some crack, had it in my mouth. I got sent back.

When I got out, I went back to Milestone and I couldn't get no job, so I was hustling. I'm not gonna walk around begging, dirty, homeless when every one else in America is eating. I was doing the smallest crimes so I'd do the less time. I passed a few $2 bills for twenties. Whenever I got a twenty, I'd tear a couple of corners off and then I would get some $2 bills from the bank. Most people never see a $2 bill. So you glue the 20 on it and you just hand it to somebody and keep talking to them while they get your change. If they give you change for a twenty, well, they gave it to you, you didn't tell them it was a twenty. But I tried to pass one in this little store and this Chinese lady followed me out on to the street and started yelling. I got busted again.

Now I been out since last month. I'm living in the FAD [Freedom Against Drugs] program out on 48th Ave. I'm getting GA. I get $172 every two weeks. They help you get on welfare. I'm goin to go to the Northern California Service League to see Nancy Lopez. She tries to get ex's a job. I'm gonna get a job, save me some money, become a functioning citizen of society.

Dereliction. Most of those who do not find a rare niche in some conventional or marginal realm steadily gravitate to the world of the homeless street people who live from day to day, drinking, hanging out, and surviving (but not for too many years) by making the rounds of soup kitchens and homeless shelters. A recent study of homelessness by Martha Burt found that 80 percent of the homeless population have been in jail, prison, or a mental hospital.[27] We believe that a followup study (which has not been done) of prisoners after release would reveal that more than 25 percent eventually end up on the streets, where they live out a short life of dereliction, alcoholism, and drug abuse. A 43-year-old black man we interviewed appeared to have become a derelict.

I been violated three times. Twice for absconding, once for a dirty drug test. I've been to the county jail four times. I was in a substance abuse program for a little while.

One time I had a little job for a while as a janitor in a machine shop. They fired me. Said I had a drinking problem. Now I'm living on the street. I just got out of an alcohol program. I stay at the shelters when I can. You sign up and they have a lottery. I'm getting welfare and am waiting for a room

> through the Tenderloin Housing. As soon as I get a room, I can clean up and keep my clothes clean and get a little job. Been staying away from Safeway, stealing booze. I'm determined to stay out this time. I've been to the shelter on 5th and Bryant, a multiple service center for the homeless. They're gonna develop a job around my skills, fix my rèsumé.

Generally speaking, this is a very grave situation. Some ex-prisoners, with luck, resolve, and some help, do all right. But most of those who eventually stay out of prison do not live successful or gratifying lives by their or conventional society's standards. They remain dependent on others or the state, drift back and forth from petty crime to subsistence, menial, dependent living, or gravitate to the new permanent urban underclass—the "homeless." Many die relatively young: "I started getting real nervous. Most of the guys I ran with were dead from AIDS, shot, drugs, or whatever."[28]

Imprisonment is not the total cause of this depressing outcome, but its contribution is considerable. Any imprisonment reduces the opportunities of felons, most of whom had relatively few opportunities to begin with. Doing time in the new generation of warehouse prisons, in which routinization and isolation have increased and rehabilitative efforts have all but completely disappeared, only makes matters worse.

NOTES

1. The federal government uses the category "conditional release" to represent inmates released to parole supervision either at the discretion of a parole board or as a requirement of the inmate's sentence, and releases to probation. The latter instance reflects sentences where the court has the authority to place an inmate on probation after serving a brief period of incarceration at a state prison. Generally, this practice is referred to as "shock incarceration" and includes the recent interest in boot camps.
2. U.S. Department of Justice, Bureau of Justice Statistics, *National Corrections Reporting Program, 1989* (Washington, D.C.: U.S. Government Printing Office, 1992, p. 28.
3. The rate at which parole boards grant parole at the first release date varies dramatically by the type of crime the inmate was

sentenced to prison for and from state to state. Parole boards in general, however, do not release the majority of inmates eligible for parole at the inmate's first hearing.

4. California Department of Corrections, *California Prisoners and Parolees, 1991* (Sacramento, Calif.: Department of Corrections, 1993), p. 7-1; personal correspondence with Robin Bates, Chief, Classification and Planning, Nevada Department of Prisons, Inmate Classification and Planning Division, Carson City, NV.
5. California Department of Corrections, *California Prisoners and Parolees, 1991* (Sacramento, Calif.: Department of Corrections, 1993), table 36A.
6. James Austin, *Reforming Florida's Unjust, Costly, and Ineffective Sentencing Laws* (San Francisco, Calif.: National Council on Crime and Delinquency, 1993).
7. U.S. Department of Justice, Bureau of Justice Statistics, *Recidivism of Prisoners Released in 1983* (Washington, D.C.: U.S. Government Printing Office, April 1989).
8. James Austin, "Using Early Release to Relieve Prison Crowding: A Dilemma in Public Policy," *Crime and Delinquency* 32, 4 (October 1986): 404–503; Joan Petersilia, Susan Turner, and Joyce Peterson, *Prison versus Probation in California: The Implications for Crime and Offender Recidivism* (Santa Monica, Calif.: The Rand Corporation, July 1986).
9. Petersilia, Turner, and Peterson, *Prison versus Probation* (Santa Monica, Calif.: The Rand Corporation, July 1986).
10. James Austin, *Parole Outcome in California: The Consequences of Determinate Sentencing, Punishment, and Incapacitation on Parole Performance* (San Francisco, Calif.: National Council on Crime and Delinquency, 1989).
11. James Austin, *The Effectiveness of Reduced Prison Terms on Public Safety and Costs: Evaluation of the Illinois Supplemental Meritorious Good-Time Program* (San Francisco, Calif.: National Council on Crime and Delinquency, 1993).
12. U.S. Department of Justice, Bureau of Justice Statistics, *The Prevalence of Imprisonment* (Washington, D.C.: U.S. Government Printing Office, July 1985).

13. James Austin, Aaron McVey, and Fred Richer, *Correctional Options for the State of Nevada to Constrain Prison Population Growth,* San Francisco, Calif.: National Council on Crime and Delinquency, 1993.
14. This sample was not randomly determined. We had requested permission from the California Department of Corrections to conduct a far more systematic study that would have entailed a more rigorous design. However, the request to have access to lists of parolees was refused by the director. Faced with this obstacle, we decided to distribute ten fliers to persons waiting in line for a free lunch at the Glide Memorial Methodist Church in San Francisco. The fliers stated we were seeking parolees to be interviewed and that we would pay $20 per interview. We were flooded with respondents and had to refuse to take any more after four days of interviewing. It should be noted that there are over 85,000 parolees on supervision in California.
15. John Irwin, *The Felon* (Englewood Cliffs, N.J.: Prentice-Hall, 1970), pp. 113–114.
16. Richard Berk and David Rauma, "Remuneration and Recidivism: The Long-Term Impact of Unemployment Compensation on Ex-Offenders," *Journal of Quantitative Criminology* 3, 1 (1987): 3–27.
17. These figures were supplied by the California Department of Corrections Research Branch, 1993.
18. From interviews conducted by staff at the Center on Juvenile and Criminal Justice, San Francisco, California, reported in their "Parole Violators in California: A Waste of Money, A Waste of Time" (September 1991), p. 8. Actually, the typical caseload of a California parole agent is 75.
19. Based on the extremely high violation rate, the California Department of Corrections has initiated several reforms designed to lower the technical violation rate. As of 1993, the rate had indeed declined to under 40 percent for all inmates released to parole supervision.
20. Austin, *Parole Outcome in California,* p. 20.
21. Joan Petersilia and Susan Turner, "An Evaluation of Intensive Probation in California," *The Journal of Criminal Law and Criminology* 82, 3 (Fall 1991): 610–658.

22. J. R. Lilly, "Tagging Reviewed," *The Howard Journal* 24, 4 (1990): 229–244.
23. U. S. Department of Justice, Bureau of Justice Statistics, *Correctional Populations in the United States, 1989* (Washington, D.C.: U.S. Government Printing Office, October 1991).
24. James Austin and Patricia Hardyman, *The Use of Early Parole with Electronic Monitoring to Control Prison Crowding* (San Francisco: National Council on Crime and Delinquency, 1992); Terry L. Baumer and Robert I. Mendelsohn, *Final Report: The Electronic Monitoring of Non-Violent Convicted Felons: An Experiment in Home Detention* (Indianapolis: School of Public and Environmental Affairs, Indiana University, January, 1990).
25. Excerpts from quotes included in Chapter 3.
26. According to the U.S. Department of Justice, 64 percent of all prison releases to parole had less than a high school education, with a median education level at the tenth grade. The tenth grade level is the same for prison admissions, indicating the absence of any improvement in education level while imprisoned (U.S. Department of Justice, Bureau of Justice Statistics, *National Corrections Reporting Program, 1989* [Washington, D.C.: U.S. Government Printing Office, November 1992]).
27. Martha Burt, *Over the Edge* (New York: Urban Institute and Russell Sage Foundation, 1992).
28. Interview, 51-year-old parolee, San Francisco, April 1993.

6

It's About Time

Our study of the American prison system revealed that most of the unprecedented numbers of people we are sending to prison are guilty of petty property and drug crimes or violations of their conditions of probation or parole. Their crimes or violations lack any of the elements that the public believes are serious or associates with dangerous criminals. Even offenders who commit frequent felonies and who define themselves as "outlaws," "dope fiends," crack dealers, or "gang bangers" commit mostly petty felonies. These "high-rate" offenders, as they have been labeled by policy makers and criminologists, are, for the most part, uneducated, unskilled (at crime as well as conventional pursuits), and highly disorganized persons who have no access to any form of rewarding, meaningful conventional life. They usually turn to dangerous, mostly unrewarding, petty criminal pursuits as one of the few options they have to earn money, win some respect, and avoid monotonous lives on the streets. Frequently, they spend most of their young lives behind bars.

What may be more surprising is that a majority of all persons sent to prison, even the high-rate offenders, aspire to a relatively modest conventional life and hope to prepare for that while serving their prison sentences. This should be considered particularly important because very little in the way of equipping prisoners for a conventional life on the outside is occurring in our prisons. In preceding decades, particularly the 1950s and 1960s, a much greater effort was made to "rehabilitate" prisoners. Whatever the outcome of these efforts (as this is a matter of some dispute), rehabilitation has been all but abandoned.[1] Prisons have been redefined as places of punishment. In addition, rapid expansion has crowded prisoners into physically inadequate institutions and siphoned off most available funds from all services other than those required to maintain control. Prisons have become true human warehouses—often highly crowded, violent, and cruel.

THE FINANCIAL COST

We must consider the costs and benefits of increased imprisonment rates. The financial cost is the easiest to estimate. Most people are aware that prisons are expensive to build and operate. Few, however, understand just how expensive. Indeed, previous estimates routinely cited by public officials have dramatically underestimated the amounts of money spent on housing prisoners and building new prisons.

Prison and jail administrators typically calculate operating costs by dividing their annual budget by the average daily prison population. However, this accounting practice is misleading and produces patently low estimates of the true costs of imprisonment. For example, agency budgets often exclude contracted services for food, medical care, legal services, and transportation provided by other government agencies. According to two studies conducted in New York, these additional expenses increased the official operating costs by 20 to 25 percent.[2] An independent audit of the Indiana prison system found that actual expenditures were one-third higher than those reported by the agency.[3] Besides these "hidden" direct expenditures, there are other costs that are rarely included in such calculations. To name only a few, the state loses taxes that could be paid by many of the imprisoned, pays more welfare to their families, and maintains spacious prison grounds that are exempt from state and local real estate taxation. In the New York study conducted by Coopers and Lybrand in 1977, these costs amounted to over $21,000 per prisoner.[4]

Although there is considerable variation among the states, on the average prison officials claim that it costs about $20,000 per year to house, feed, clothe, and supervise a prisoner.[5] Because this estimate does not include indirect costs, the true annual expenditure probably exceeds $30,000 per prisoner.

The other enormous cost is prison construction. Prisons are enclosed, "total" institutions in which prisoners are not only housed, but guarded, fed, clothed, and worked. They also receive some schooling and medical and psychological treatment. These needs require—in addition to cellblocks or dormitories—infirmaries, classrooms, laundries, offices, maintenance shops, boiler rooms, and kitchens. Dividing the total construction costs of one of these institutions by the number of prisoners it houses produces a cost per "bed" of as low as $7,000 for a minimum-security prison to $155,000 for a maximum-security prison.

Instead of using current tax revenues to pay directly for this construction, however, the state does what most citizens do when they buy a house—that is, borrow the money, which must be paid back over several decades. The borrowing is done by selling bonds or using other financing instruments that may triple the original figure. The costs of prison construction are further increased by errors in original bids by contractors and cost overruns caused by delays in construction, which seem to be the rule rather than the exception. A recent survey of 15 states with construction projects revealed that cost overruns averaged *40 percent* of the original budget projections.[6]

Consequently, when a state builds and finances a typical medium-security prison, it will spend approximately $268,000 per bed for construction alone. So in the states that have expanded their prison populations, the cost per additional prisoner will be $39,000 a year. This includes the cost of building the new cell amortized 30 years. In other words, the 30-year cost of adding space for one prisoner is more than $1 million.

These enormous increases in the cost of imprisonment are just beginning to be felt by the states. Budgetary battles in which important state services for children, the elderly, the sick, and the poor are gutted to pay for prisons have already begun. In coming years, great cutbacks in funds for public education, medical services for the poor, highway construction, and other state services will occur.

CRIME REDUCTION

Those who are largely responsible for this state of affairs—elected officials who have harangued on the street crime issue and passed laws resulting in more punitive sentencing policies, judges who deliver more and longer prison terms, and government criminal justice functionaries who have supported the punitive trend in criminal justice policies—promised that the great expansion of prison populations would reduce crime in our society. A key U.S. Department of Justice official recently summarized the government's scientific basis for supporting incarceration as the best means for reducing crime as follows: "Statisticians and criminal justice researchers have consistently found that falling crime rates are associated with rising imprisonment rates, and rising crime rates are associated with falling imprisonment rates."[7] Former Attorney General William Barr more recently restated this position, arguing that the country had a "clear choice" of either building more prisons or tolerating higher violent crime rates. This view implies that increasing the government's capacity to imprison is the single most effective strategy for reducing crime.

To support the proposition that increases in incarceration reduce crime, senior U.S. Department of Justice officials have compared Uniform Crime Reports (UCR) violent crime rates (homicides, robbery, assault, rape, and kidnapping) with imprisonment rates between 1960 and 1990 in ten-year increments (see Figure 6-1).[8] By selectively using these ten-year increments, the Justice Department's bar chart shows that, during the 1960s, imprisonment rates dropped by 19 percent while reported violent crime rates *increased* 104 percent. During the 1970s violent crime rates continued to *increase* again, but by only 47 percent, whereas imprisonment rates increased by 39 percent. And in the 1980s, as imprisonment rates increased by 99 percent, violent crimes rates again *increased,* but by only 11 percent.

In other words, although violent crimes rates have *steadily increased* over the past three decades, the rates of increase were lowest during the 1980s, when imprisonment rates were at their highest levels. These data have led a Justice Department spokesperson to claim that violent crime will decline even more if more persons are imprisoned.

> No one knows for sure what the 1990s will bring. But my guess, based on the lessons learned over the past three decades, is this: If imprisonment rates continue to rise, overall violent crime rates will not increase and could actually fall in the 1990s. A big "if," of course, is whether imprisonment rates will continue their steady upward climb.[9]

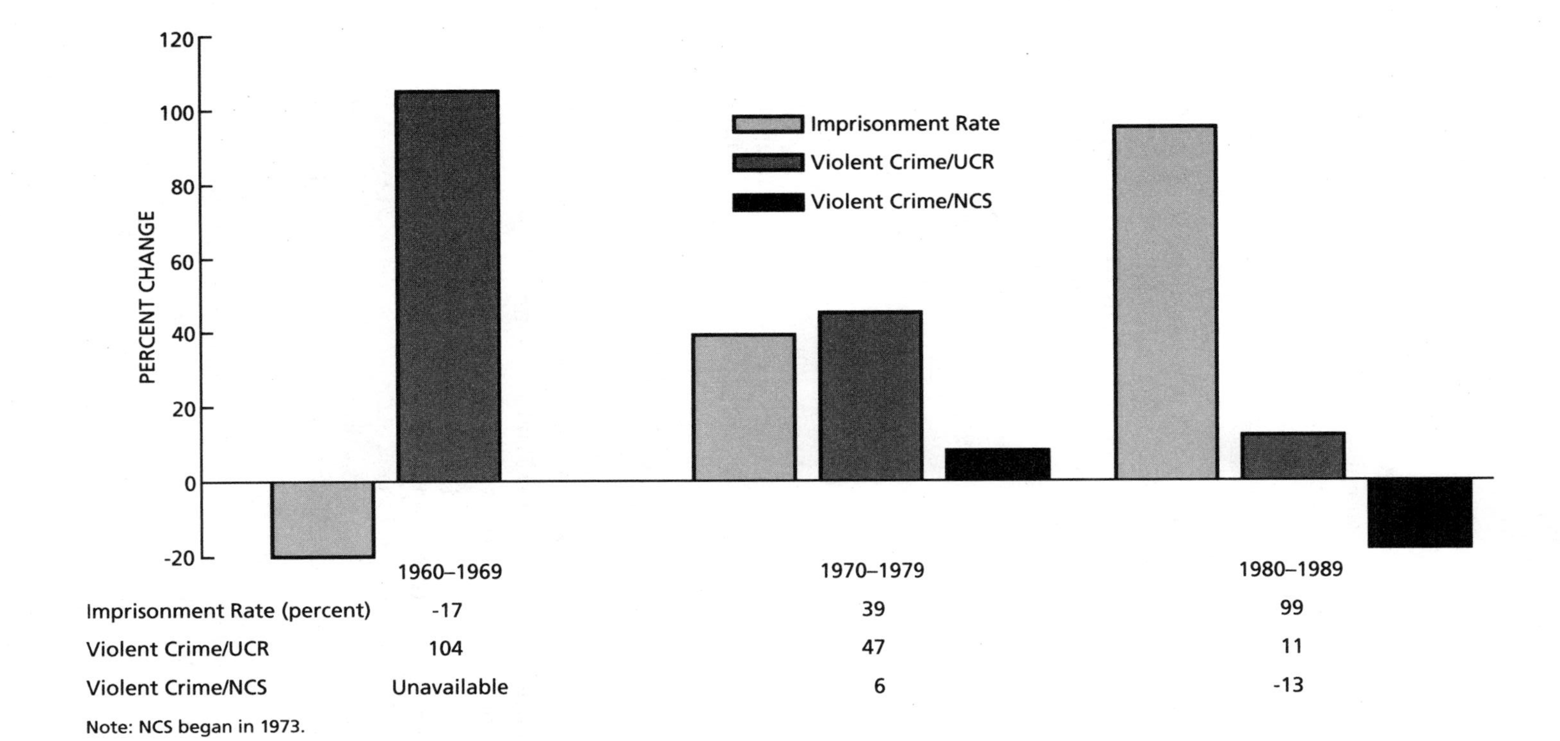

	1960–1969	1970–1979	1980–1989
Imprisonment Rate (percent)	-17	39	99
Violent Crime/UCR	104	47	11
Violent Crime/NCS	Unavailable	6	-13

Note: NCS began in 1973.

Source: William Barr, *Combatting Violent Crime: 24 Recommendations to Strengthen Criminal Justice*, Washington, D.C.: U.S. Department of Justice, Office of the Attorney General, p. 5.

FIGURE 6-1 Imprisonment and Violent Crime Rates, 1960s, 1970s, and 1980s

We suggested in Chapter 1 that these arguments are invalid and that there has been no increase in public safety produced by the imprisonment binge. On the contrary, a careful examination of all available information supports the conclusion that more imprisonment has not had any significant impact on crime rates. Most tellingly, crime rates have not declined despite the massive increases in prison and jail populations. Figure 6-2 summarizes the percent changes in UCR crime rates and imprisonment rates from 1960 to 1991.

Returning to the argument set forth by the U.S. Department of Justice that crime rate increases were lowest in the decade of the 1980s and highest in the 1960s, a more careful year-by-year analysis of the same UCR data cited by the Justice Department shows that the nation's overall crime rates have had relative periods of stabilization in all three decades (1960–1962, 1970–1973, 1975–1978, and 1980-1984) only to be followed by crime rate increases despite increases in the use of imprisonment (Figure 6-2). For the imprisonment theory to be valid, these countervailing trends should either not have occurred or should somehow be explained by the imprisonment theory. If there was a direct causal relationship between imprisonment and crime rates, stabilization in crime rates during these time periods should not take place.

The imprisonment advocates also claim that crime has been reduced since 1973 by over 25 percent, with most of the decline occurring since 1980. They have based their case *exclusively* on the 1973–1991 NCVS household surveys. Figure 6-3 summarizes the UCR, NCVS, and imprisonment rates between 1973 and 1991—the time period for which all three measures have been recorded by the Justice Department.

During this same time period, imprisonment rates more than *tripled,* from 98 to 310 per 100,000. Despite this increase, both UCR property and violent crime rates actually *increased* by 82 percent and 38 percent, respectively. There was a decline in UCR rates between 1980 and 1984, only to be followed by a steady increase thereafter. Like the UCR rates, the NCVS data also show a decline in household reported crime beginning in 1980.

Imprisonment advocates initially heralded the 1980–1984 decrease in both the UCR and NCVS crime rates while imprisonment rates grew from 138 to 179 per 100,000 as proof that imprisonment reduces crime. Beginning in 1985, however, the UCR crime rate began to increase despite the fact that the imprisonment rate continued to

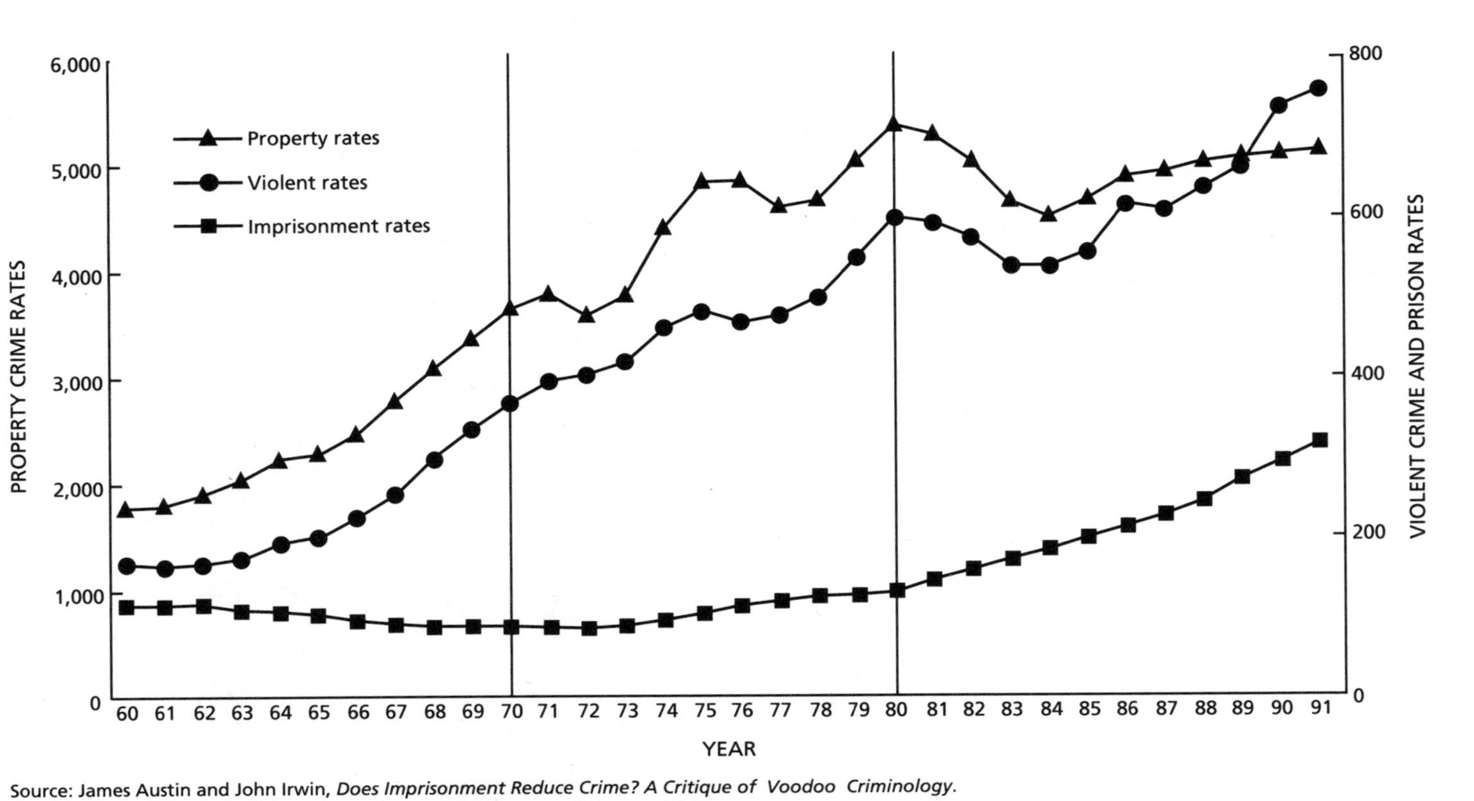

Source: James Austin and John Irwin, *Does Imprisonment Reduce Crime? A Critique of Voodoo Criminology*. San Francisco, Calif. National Council on Crime and Delinquency, February, 1993.

FIGURE 6-2 Annual Changes in UCR, Crime and Prison Rates

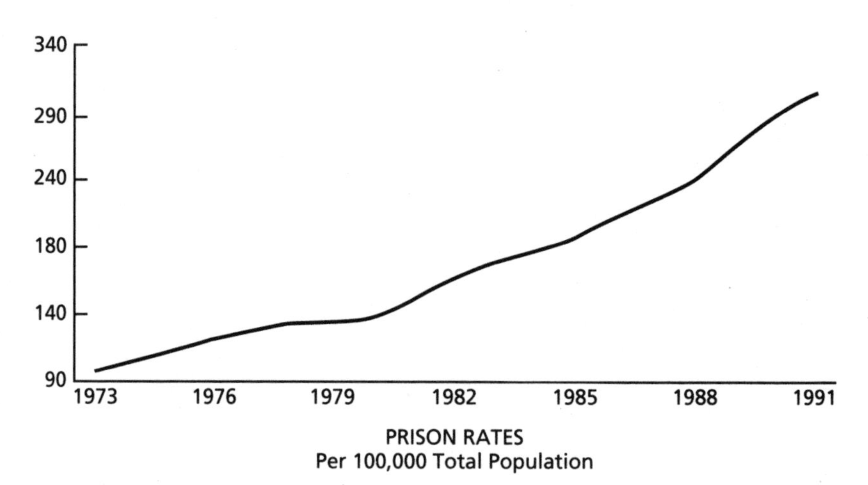

FIGURE 6-3a Comparisons of Prison, UCR, and NCVS Trends, 1973–1991

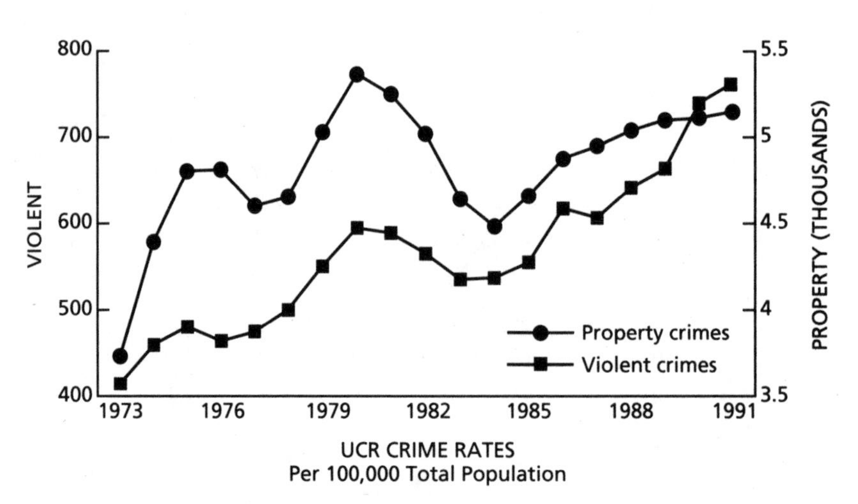

FIGURE 6-3b Comparisons of Prison, UCR, and NCVS Trends, 1973–1991

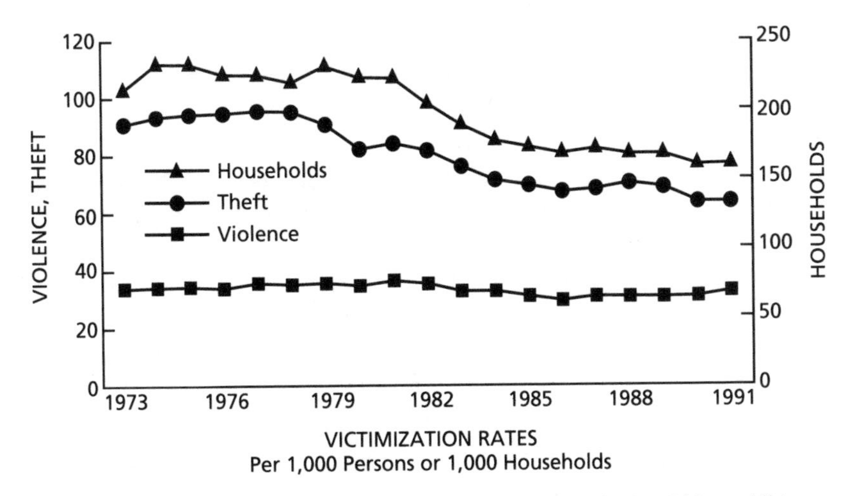

Source: James Austin and John Irwin, *Does Imprisonment Reduce Crime? A Critique of "Voodoo" Criminology.* San Francisco, CA: National Council on Crime and Delinquency, February, 1993.

FIGURE 6-3c Comparisons of Prison, UCR, and NCVS Trends, 1973–1991

escalate. Only the NCVS overall rates continued to decline through 1991. Even for the NCVS data, however, there has been virtually no decline in violent crime rates. In fact, since 1986, the NCVS violent crime rate has *increased* 11 percent, from 28.1 to 31.3. Only property theft and household burglary as reported by the NCVS have shown declines (see Figure 6-3).

Demographic Shifts and Crime Rates. There are several reasons to question the interpretation that reductions for NCVS property crimes validate the "imprisonment reduces crime" perspective. First is the failure to incorporate the influence of shifting demographics on crime rates. Most crimes are committed by males between the ages of 15 and 24. As that population grows or subsides, one can expect associated fluctuations in the crime rates. Before changes in crime rates can be attributed to changes in imprisonment rates, the influence of demographic changes must be taken into consideration.

Beginning in the early 1960s, the size of this age group began to grow and continued to grow through the 1970s—the exact period of the rise in crime rates (Figure 6-3). By the late 1970s, this age group as a percentage of the population began to decline and the crime rate began to ebb by 1980. A recent article by two criminologists found that most of the decline in crime rates observed since 1979–1985 was a direct result of a declining "at-risk" population. When we take into account the influence of this demographic shift, reductions in the NCVS from 1980 to 1988 are largely attributable (60 percent of the crime reduction explained) to reductions in the ages 15–24 high-crime-rate population. The same analysis, when applied to the UCR data, actually shows an increase in UCR during the same time period.[10]

The NCVS rates are also influenced by significant changes that have occurred over the past two decades in the number, characteristics, and location of U.S. households. In the most recent publication on NCVS, the Justice Department acknowledged that, since 1973, the size of the American household has (1) declined, (2) shifted from urban areas to suburban locations, and (3) shifted from the Northeast and Midwest to the South and the West.[11]

The first two conditions automatically reduce crime rate estimates because smaller households located in suburban areas are less likely than larger and urban households to experience crime. The third condition, relocation to the West where crime rates are highest, increases the likelihood of households being victimized. These trends in the NCVS must be more carefully analyzed before conclusions can be made that a tripling of the imprisonment rate is solely responsible for declines in personal and household theft.

Drug Trafficking and Property Crime. A second reason to question the drop in NCVS and UCR property crimes since 1980 is related to the dramatic increase in drug trafficking that began in 1980. It is very possible that the decline in burglary and theft reflected a change in criminal activity from these crimes to the more lucrative and less difficult drug trade business. It is difficult to prove with statistics that this shift has indeed occurred because drug dealing is not reported by the NCVS. But for those criminologists who spend time observing America's deteriorating inner cities, it is obvious that street crime has shifted from household burglaries to drug trafficking.[12]

Prison Versus Other Forms of Punishment. Even if the NCVS figures reflect a true drop in property crime, it cannot be concluded that imprisonment was the cause of the decline. As shown earlier in

Table 1-1, other and less punitive forms of correctional supervision (probation, parole, and jail populations) grew just as fast as the prison population. Statistically and substantively, it could be argued that NCVS crime rate reductions were related to greater use of probation and short jail terms since they are applied to a far larger number of offenders than prison.

State-by-State Comparisons. The *best* test of the proposition that increasing prison populations has reduced crime is a comparison between the 50 states and the District of Columbia, which serve as experiments on this issue. This is because they not only differ in their crime and imprisonment rates, but they have also undergone dramatically different changes in these over the last fifteen years.

The period 1980 to 1991 is ideal for this comparison. The national crime rate peaked in 1980, as it did individually in all but 13 states. (These peaked in 1981 or 1982.) Also, after increasing slowly for several years, the national rate of incarceration began to rise steeply (see Figure 6-3). All the states increased their prison populations in that 12-year period, but they did so by very different amounts, from 26 to 742 per 100,000. The states and D.C., in a sense, are 51 different "petri dishes" (used in biological experiments), each with its unique array of factors that could be related to changes in crime rates, into which the experimental variable—increases in imprisonment—is introduced. If a causal relationship existed, we would see a consistent pattern—namely, states that increased their imprisonment rates the most would show the largest reductions in crime rates. Conversely, states that increased their imprisonment rates more slowly would show higher increases in crime rates.

Actually, there is no pattern. Figure 6-4 divides the states into three categories—those that increased their rates of imprisonment by less than 100, by 100 to 200, and by more than 200 per 100,000.

Most states (34) experienced a decline in crime rates. However, there is no tendency for those that increased their prison populations the most to have greater decreases in crime. In fact, the opposite is true. The states that increased their prison populations by less 100 per 100,000 were more likely to have experienced a decrease in crime than those that increased imprisonment rates by more than 200.

In Figure 6-5, the states and D. C. are plotted by their increases in rates of incarceration and changes in crime rates. If the plot converged

FIGURE 6-4 State by State Comparisons of Increases in Rates of Crime and Incarceration From 1980 to 1991 (Increases in Rates of Incarceration per 100,000)

CRIME INCREASED		
Less than 100	**100 to 200**	**More than 200**
1676* Texas (87**)	1364 Ark. (186)	971 Louisiana (255)
1248 N. Car. (26)	889 Georgia (123)	804 Miss. (203)
869 Tenn. (74)	857 Ill. (152)	704 S. Carolina (235)
700 N. Mex. (85)	155 Kansas (124)	616 Oklahoma (263)
111 W. Vir. (18)	145 Florida (138)	532 Wash. D.C. (742)
49 Neb. (57)		432 Alabama (243)

CRIME DECREASED		
Less than 100	**100 to 200**	**More than 200**
– 170 N. Dakota (40)	– 13 Virginia (136)	– 509 Alaska (201)
– 273 Utah (85)	– 17 Missouri (179)	– 538 Mich. (202)
– 304 Minn. (29)	– 76 Kentucky (162)	– 766 Arizona (238)
– 333 Wisconsin (73)	– 122 Indiana (112)	– 908 Delaware (159)
– 600 Maine (66)	– 164 S. Dakota (102)	– 970 N. Jersey (224)
– 611 Washington (77)	– 177 Penn. (124)	–1060 Calif. (222)
– 613 Iowa (58)	– 398 Ohio (198)	–2555 Nevada (247)
– 758 Mass. (94)	– 421 Maryland (183)	
–1034 Vermont (58)	– 518 Conn. (194)	
–1232 N. Hamp. (97)	– 586 Idaho (125)	
–1377 Montana (88)	– 597 Wyoming (112)	
	– 667 New York (196)	
	– 894 R. Island (107)	
	– 932 Oregon (109)	
	–1260 Colorado (151)	
	–1513 Hawaii (107)	

* Changes in crime rates
** Changes in rates of incarceration

Sources: *Sourcebook of Criminal Justice Statistics, 1992,* U.S. Bureau of Criminal Justice Statistics, U.S. Department of Justice and Uniform Crime Reports, 1981 to 1992, Federal Bureau of Investigation, U.S. Department of Justice.

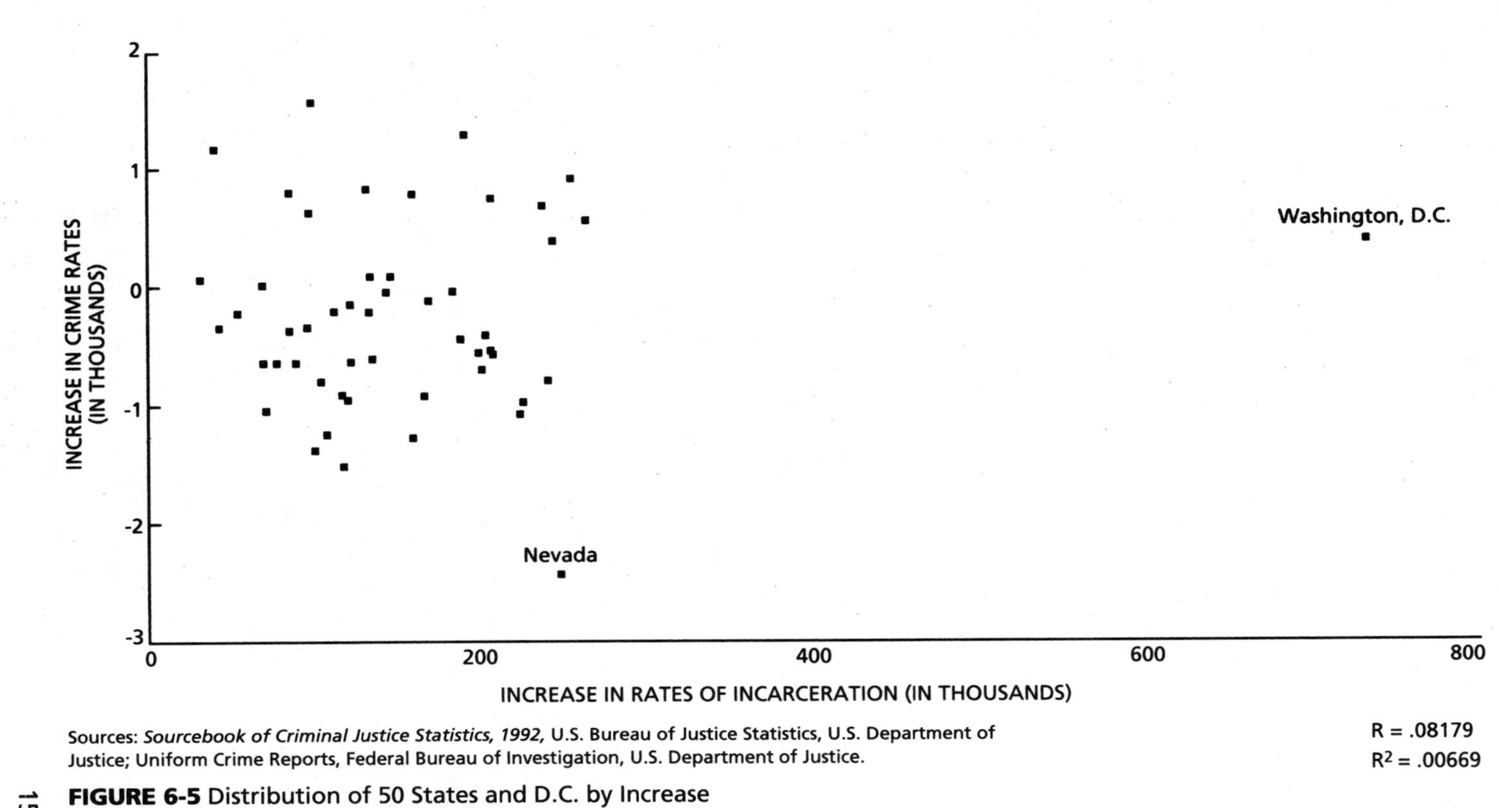

Sources: *Sourcebook of Criminal Justice Statistics, 1992,* U.S. Bureau of Justice Statistics, U.S. Department of Justice; Uniform Crime Reports, Federal Bureau of Investigation, U.S. Department of Justice.

FIGURE 6-5 Distribution of 50 States and D.C. by Increase in Rates of Incarceration and Crime, 1980–1991

on a line, it would indicate a relationship. It is apparent that there is no convergence and that greater increases in imprisonment did not produce decreases in crime. We analyzed this distribution by regression analysis, which establishes the line from which the points deviate the least (whether or not the distribution calls for a line) and measures to what extent the points deviate from it. This is indicated in a coefficient of correlation—*R*. When *R* is 1.0, the points all lie on the line. In our case, *R* was .08179 in the positive direction. This suggests that in the 12 year period, there was a very slight tendency for more incarceration to be related to *increases* in crime. It would be simple minded to conclude that this is a causal relationship. But it is very reasonable to recognize that this state by state comparison strongly indicates that the massive increases in incarceration failed to produce *any* reduction in crime rates.

The California Imprisonment Experiment. If we were to pick a state to test the imprisonment theory, California would be the obvious choice, for this state's prison population has increased from 19,623 in 1977 to over 110,000 by 1992. Former Attorney General William Barr believes California should serve as the model for the rest of the country. California, he states, "quadrupled its prison population during the 1980s and various forms of violent crimes fell by as much as 37 percent. But in Texas, which did not increase prison space, crime increased 29 percent in the decade."[13]

A closer examination of the California data presents a very different picture than that cited by Barr. Figure 6-6 summarizes percent changes in reported violent crime rates from 1981 to 1990 and California's imprisonment rates (excluding the rapidly accelerating jail population). During this period, the size of the prison population increased by 237 percent (from 29,202 to 97,309) and the jail population increased by 118 percent (34,064 to 74,312). Prison operating costs increased by 400 percent, and jail operating costs increased by 265 percent. As of 1990, Californians were paying nearly $3 billion per year to operate the state's prisons and jails.

What has been the impact of this substantial investment in violent crime? Contrary to the claim that the violent crime rate (homicide, rape, robbery, and assault) has dropped, the rate actually *increased* by 21 percent. Substantial declines did occur, but only for burglary and

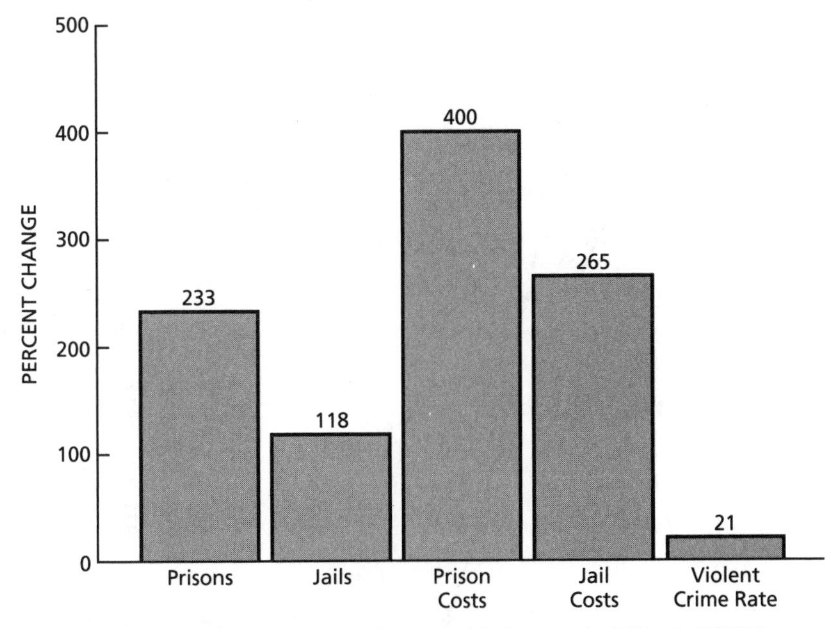

Source: California Department of Justice, "Crime and Delinquency in California,1990" Sacramento, CA: Office of Attorney General, 1991.

FIGURE 6-6 Percent Change in California's Imprisonment Experiment, 1981–1990

larceny theft—a phenomenon that, as we noted earlier, was at least partially attributable to growth in illegal drug trafficking and shifts in the at-risk population. More interesting is the fact that after 1984 the overall crime rate, and especially violent crimes and auto theft, have grown despite a continued escalation of imprisonment (Figure 6-7).

California is now so strapped for funds that it must dramatically reduce the number of its parole officers and has been unable to open two brand new prisons, capable of holding 12,000 inmates. The state now has the most overcrowded prison system in the nation (183 percent of rated capacity) and spends millions of dollars each year on court cases challenging the crowded prison conditions. Despite the billions of dollars now being spent each year in locking up offenders, the public is as fearful of crime as it was a decade ago. Clearly, the grand California imprisonment experiment has done little to reduce crime or the public's fear of crime.

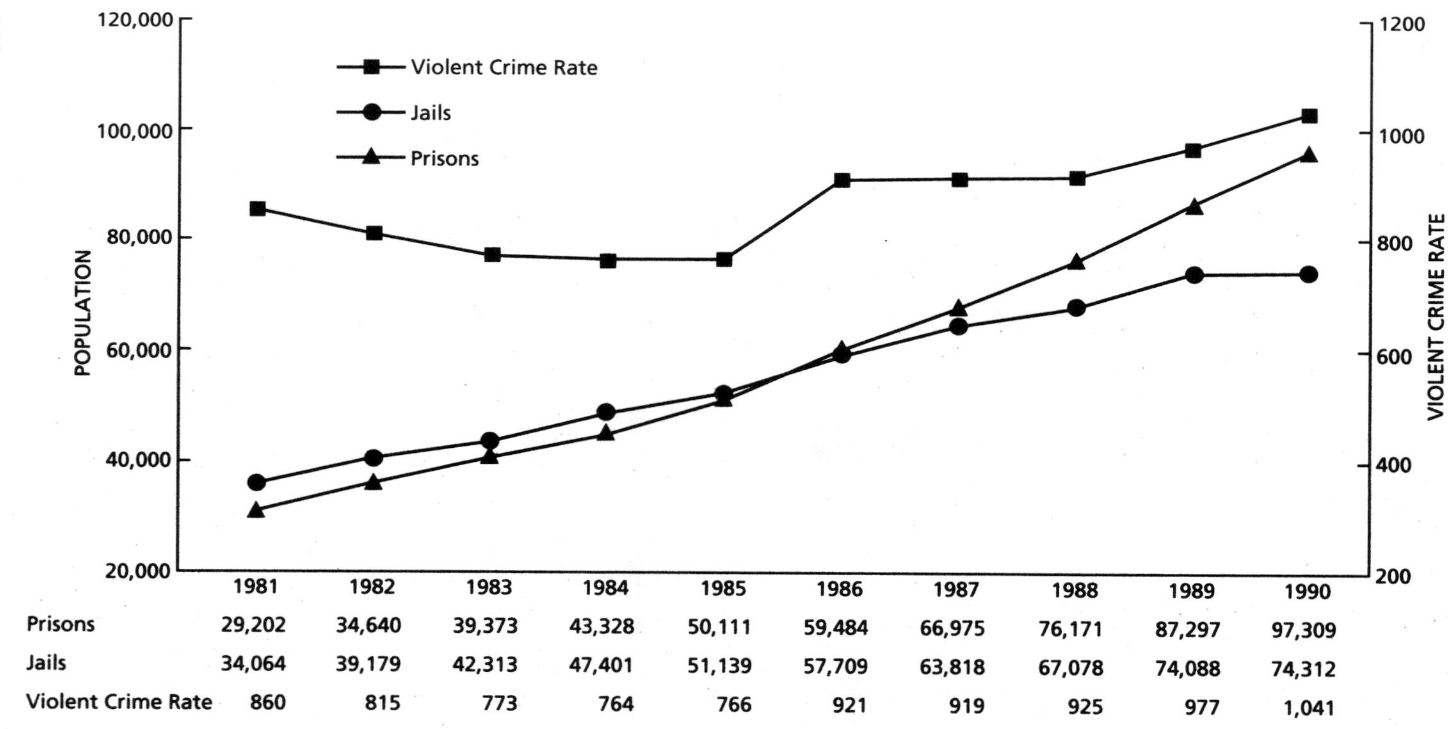

	1981	1982	1983	1984	1985	1986	1987	1988	1989	1990
Prisons	29,202	34,640	39,373	43,328	50,111	59,484	66,975	76,171	87,297	97,309
Jails	34,064	39,179	42,313	47,401	51,139	57,709	63,818	67,078	74,088	74,312
Violent Crime Rate	860	815	773	764	766	921	919	925	977	1,041

Source: California Department of Justice, "Crime and Delinquency in California, 1990," Sacramento, CA: Office of Attorney General, 1991.

FIGURE 6-7 California's Imprisonment Experiment, 1981–1990

The Costs of Further Escalating the Imprisonment Binge. Many argue that crime has not been reduced in California or nationally simply because we have not incarcerated enough persons. They suggest that if we were willing to imprison many times more people for much longer periods of time, significant reductions in crime would occur, that is, "street crime." (The pervasive and more expensive other forms of crime, e.g., white collar crime, are not and would not be affected by imprisonment.)

This viewpoint is not mere speculation but one that is being regularly advocated by many politicians. Former Attorney General William Barr listed 24 steps the government should take to reduce violent crime including "truth in sentencing" that requires inmates to serve the full amount of their sentences, increased use of mandatory minimum prison sentences, relaxation of evidentiary rules to increase conviction rates, greater use of the death penalty, and increased numbers of police officers.[14] President Clinton campaigned on adding 100,000 police officers to the streets to increase arrests. And, both political parties have formally advocated the need to get even tougher with criminals.

The consequences of such a program are presented in Table 6-1. The first column represents our current criminal justice policies while the second reflects how these numbers might change if we pursued a policy of escalating the war on crime in a manner suggested by William Barr. The major components of such a program would be as follows:

Policy 1: Add 100,000 police officers;
Result: Increases the number of felony arrests from 4.3 million to 5.0 million;[15]

Policy 2: Increase the conviction rate from 65 percent to 75 percent;[16]
Result: Increases the number of convictions from 2.3 million to 3.4 million;

Policy 3: Increase the proportion of convictions resulting in a prison sentence from 19 percent to 40 percent.[17]
Result: Increases the number of prison admissions from 475,000 to 1.5 million;

Policy 4: Adopt a "truth in sentencing" policy that would require offenders to serve 80 percent of their prison terms
Result: Length of stay in prison would increase from 1.6 years to 5 years.

TABLE 6-1 The Costs of Escalating the War on Crime

	Current	**New**
Victimizations Per Year	35 million	Unknown
Arrests	14.2 million	16.6 million
Felony Arrests	4.3 million	5.0 million
Conviction Rate	65 percent	75 percent
Convictions	2.8 million	3.75 million
Prison Sentence Rate	19 percent	40 percent
Prison Admissions	532,000	1.5 million
Sentence Length	6 years	6 years
Length of Stay	1.6 years	5 years
Prison Population	830,000	7.5 million
Additional Prison Costs:		
New Prison Beds	N/A	$376 billion
Operating Costs	$15.1 billion	$133 billion
Other Criminal Justice Costs	$58.9 billion	$88 billion
Incarceration Rate Per 100,000	310	3,015

The net result of these reforms would be to create a prison population of 7.5 million. Such a massive expansion of the prison population would undoubtedly have a profound impact on the crime rate. But there would be a heavy price to pay. An additional 6.7 million prison beds would have to be constructed at a cost of at least $376 billion.[18] Annual operating costs would escalate from $15.1 billion to $133 billion.[19]

To do this constitutionally while preserving a semblance of our civil rights would require an expansion of the other parts of the criminal justice system—the jails, courts, and police departments. Assuming that the use of probation and parole would be reduced there would be limited savings on the least expensive components of the correctional system.

The annual price of all this escalation, less the prison construction costs, would probably exceed $220 billion as opposed to the $74 billion now being spent, with most of these costs being borne by state governments to operate large scale prison systems. States now spend only $14 billion on corrections alone (which includes probation and parole services). Total state general fund expenditures in 1990 totaled $300 billion.[20] Consequently, to operate such a massive prison system at the state level would require over one third of all state revenues to be dedicated to prison operations. And these costs would not include the nearly $376 billion in capital construction funds or increases to local government to expand and operate its law enforcement, court systems, and local jails.

Unless we wanted to strip down or abandon many other government enterprises—education, welfare, transportation, medical services—we would have to greatly increase state taxes to pay for this massive experiment in imprisonment. In many ways—the financial costs, the social disruptions, the removal of a very large percent of young males—this policy would be like World War II, prolonged for decades.

Of course there would be other consequences. The nation's incarceration rate would increase from 310 per 100,000 to over 3,000 per 100,000. Since 47 percent of the current prison population is black, it would mean that most of the nation's 5.5 million black males age 18-39 would be incarcerated and we would look a lot like South Africa of the 1950s and 1960s.[21]

It is still not clear what this would do to overall crime rates. Certainly, the removal of such a large portion of young males would reduce the forms of street crime we are presently experiencing. However, it is impossible to anticipate what new forms of social problems, crime, and upheavals this punitive experiment would cause. The massive social disruptions—such as the removal of most young, black males—might result in unanticipated new types of violent, criminal activities. In a few years, millions of parolees, who probably will be considerably socially crippled and embittered by their long prison terms, will be returning to society. They will at least be an enormous nuisance and burden, but also may engage in a lot of crime. Even if we assume that crime would eventually decline, how long would we have to maintain such a large prison system to continually deter and incapacitate each successive generation of potential criminals?

Since we do not believe Americans are ready for this costly solution to the crime problem through imprisonment, we are left with its failure.

Other Factors that Cause Crime. For some reason, imprisonment advocates have completely rejected or ignored the long and rich history of criminology that has shown that many other social forces, in addition to the response of the criminal justice system, affect crime rates. We can begin with the obvious observation that America's crime rates are much higher than those of other industrialized countries. Furthermore, dramatic disparities exist among the major regions of the United States, among individual states, and among cities and less urbanized areas. What are the forces that contribute to this wide variation?

A recent study by Arnold Linsky and Murray Straus sought to explain why states have different levels of violence, crime, and mental illness.[22] They found that states with the highest crime rates ranked highest in the following social stress indicators:

1. Business failures
2. Unemployment claims
3. Workers on strike
4. Personal bankruptcies
5. Mortgage foreclosures
6. Divorces
7. Abortions
8. Illegitimate births
9. Infant deaths
10. Fetal deaths
11. Disaster assistance
12. State residency of less than five years
13. New houses authorized
14. New welfare cases
15. High school dropouts

These 15 items made up a "social stress" scale that was measured for each region and state of the United States. They found that this social stress scale is the best predictor of crime rates.

A more recent re-analysis by Robert Sampson and John Laub of the classic Sheldon and Eleanor Glueck's cohort study of 500 delinquents and 500 non-delinquents provides further evidence on the limited impact of imprisonment on criminal careers. The 1,000 youth who were residing in Massachusetts in the 1930s were tracked until age 45 to determine those factors that contributed to either an escalation or reduction in criminal behavior. In terms of factors that contributed to adult criminal behavior the researchers found that job stability and marriage sharply mitigated one's criminal activities. More significantly, whether these adults were incarcerated or not had no impact on their crime rates. The study concludes that social factors do have a very important and persistant impact on crime rates while the state's ability to punish does not.[23]

VOODOO CRIMINOLOGY

The failure of the massive expansion of prison populations to accomplish its most important objective—the reduction of crime—should come as no surprise because the idea that increased penalties will reduce crime is based on a simplistic and fallacious theory of criminal behavior. It starts with the idea that every person is an isolated, willful actor who makes completely rational decisions to maximize his or her pleasure and to minimize his or her pain. Consequently, individuals only commit crimes when they believe it will lead to more pleasure, gain, or satisfaction and with minimal risk for pain or punishment. If penalties for being caught are small or nonexistent, then many persons who are not restrained by other factors (e.g., strong conventional morals or the disapproval of close friends or family) will commit crimes—indeed, a *lot* of crimes. Only by increasing the certainty and severity of punishment, this thinking goes, will people "think twice" and be deterred.

The punishment/incapacitation/deterrence theory assumes that all individuals have access to the same conventional lifestyles for living out a law-abiding life. This is not true for most of the individuals who are caught up in our criminal justice system. For many, particularly young members of the inner-city underclass, the choice is not between conventional and illegal paths to the good life, but between illegal and risky paths or no satisfaction at all. They are faced with a limited and depressing choice between a menial, dull, impoverished, undignified life at the bottom of the conventional heap or a life with some excitement, some monetary return, and a slim chance of larger financial rewards, albeit with great risks of being imprisoned, maimed, or even killed. Consequently, many "choose" crime despite the threat of imprisonment.

For many young males, especially African Americans and Hispanics, the threat of going to prison or jail is no threat at all but rather an expected or accepted part of life. Most minority males will be punished by the criminal justice system during their lifetime. Deterrence and punishment are effective only when the act of punishment actually worsens a person's lifestyle. For millions of males, imprisonment poses no such threat. As a young black convict put it when Claude Brown told him that his preprison life meant that there was a "60 percent chance he will be killed, permanently maimed, or end up doing a long bit in jail":

> "I see where you comin' from, Mr. Brown," he replied, "but you got things kind of turned around the wrong way. You see, all the things that you say could happen to me is dead on the money and that is why I can't lose. Look at it from my point of view for a minute. Let's say I go and get wiped [killed]. Then I ain't got no more needs, right? All my problems are solved. I don't need no more money, no more nothing, right? Okay, supposin' I get popped, shot in the spine and paralyzed for the rest of my life—that could happen playing football, you know. Then I won't need a whole lot of money because I won't be able to go no place and do nothin', right?
>
> "So, I'll be on welfare, and the welfare check is all the money I'll need, right? Now if I get busted and end up in the joint [prison] pullin' a dime and a nickel, like I am, then I don't have to worry about no bucks, no clothes. I get free rent and three squares a day. So you see, Mr. Brown, I really can't lose."[24]

AMERICA'S FARM SYSTEM FOR CRIMINALS

Most people who engage in crime do so not as isolated individuals, but—like we all are—as participants in various social organizations, groups, or "social systems," each of which has its own rules and values. Some groups in our society (often because of subjection to reduced circumstances such as poverty, idleness, and incarceration over an extended period of time) develop preferences for deviant lifestyles. For example, young males who were abused as children, dropped out of school, lived in poverty, abused drugs, and served many juvenile jail and prison sentences have become immersed in deviant values and are distanced from any set of conventional values. They are most satisfied when engaging in specialized deviant practices related to their unique culture—wild partying involving drug use and sex along with extremely risky behavior involving extreme displays of machismo.[25]

Since crime is not the sole product of individual motives, efforts, especially by the state, to punish the individual without addressing the social forces that produced that individual will fail. Individuals do not decide to sell drugs, purchase drugs, and set up single-proprietor operations on their own. Most street crime involves groups, organizations, and networks. Drug dealers are persons who have been involved in groups and networks of people who use drugs, have connections, know or are dealers. The same is true of gang bangers, hustlers, and thieves.

In effect, America has created a lower-class culture designed to produce new cohorts of street criminals each generation. Similar to organized sports, most of these criminal operations have major leagues, minors leagues, and a bench. Children come up through the ranks, learn the game, and finally move into the starting lineup once they reach their adolescent years. When they are temporarily or permanently removed (that is, arrested, imprisoned, or killed), they are replaced by others from the bench to continue the game. When the bench is depleted, someone comes up from the minors. Much as in professional and college sports, the span of their career is short, with their most active crime years taking place between the ages of 15 and 24.

Our impoverished inner-city neighborhoods (or what is left of them as neighborhoods) have almost unlimited reserves milling about who are kept out of the starting lineup by managers and first-string players. As soon as the police arrest the "kingpin" drug dealer, the leaders of a gang, some of the top pimps or hustlers, new recruits move in to take over these positions.

This characterization of criminal operations also explains why the War on Drugs, which has been going on for at least a decade, has failed. During the 1980s, the government spent billions of tax dollars and arrested millions for drug possession or drug trafficking. Regularly, the media reported that a new large-scale drug operation and some kingpin drug dealers have been caught. Drugs continue to be at least as available as they were before the new arrests, however, as "new" kingpins quickly and often violently replace the recently departed leaders.

Even if a particular type of criminal operation dies out, new crime games appear. In the late 1980s, the news media and government officials were blaming crack cocaine dealing for unprecedented numbers of homicides in Los Angeles inner city neighborhoods. However, sociologist Jack Katz discovered that, contrary to the media's reports, homicide rates in the crack neighborhoods had not changed over the last decade.[26] Earlier in the 1980s, rival gangs were killing each other over territory. It seems, using the sport analogy, that the number of players available for crime games is related to broader social conditions, such as the existence of a large underemployed population of young males who have the ordinary youthful desires for respect, excitement, and gratification but are confronted with extremely limited access to legitimate means of acquiring them. Thus, the number of potential players remains constant over an extended period. Only the types of games being played change from season to season.

CUTTING OUR LOSSES ON THE PRISON SOLUTION

The past decade has witnessed the uncritical adoption of a national policy to reduce crime by increasing the use of imprisonment. That policy has failed. Despite a more than doubling of the correctional industrial complex and a tripling of criminal justice system costs, crime in general has not been reduced. Though there is evidence that property crimes committed against households have declined, all measures of crime are increasing. Moreover, it appears that crime is likely to increase in the near future. This is not news to the American public, which is increasingly apprehensive about personal safety even as their taxes are increased to pay for the failed imprisonment policy.

For these reasons, the grand imprisonment experiment, which has dominated America's crime reduction policy for the past 15 years, should not only be severely questioned but abandoned. It has simply failed to produce its primary objective—reduced crime. This is not to say that certain offenders should not be imprisoned and, in some cases, for lengthy periods; a few individuals are truly dangerous and need to receive long sentences. But to argue that all offenders should be so treated is misguided and ineffective.

Reducing crime means addressing those factors that are more directly related to crime. This means reducing teenage pregnancies, high school dropout rates, unemployment, drug abuse, and lack of meaningful job opportunities. Although many will differ on how best to address these factors, the first step is to acknowledge that these forces have far more to do with reducing crime than escalating the use of imprisonment.

The "prison reduces crime" theory has not worked. Crime, especially violent crime, is not declining. We need to cut our losses and try crime prevention policies that will work. It may well take a decade before the fruits of such an effort are realized, but we can no longer afford to keep investing in a widespread crime reduction policy that has failed so ubiquitously.

THE SOCIAL COSTS OF IMPRISONMENT

The full range and depth of the social costs, which are tremendous, are much more difficult to identify and measure accurately. Though most of the persons in our sample were not contributing significantly to the support of a family, some were. About 40 percent indicated that they were employed at the time of arrest and 25 percent stated that they had been employed most of the time in the period before arrest. Many prisoners sent to prison are married and have children. Moreover, all of them have mothers, fathers, brothers, sisters, uncles, aunts, or cousins. Though it is sometimes true that a prisoner was causing family and friends a great deal of difficulty, usually relatives experience some disruption and pain when persons are sent to prison. The removal of an individual from his social contexts does some harm to his family, friends, and employer, though the amount of this harm is hard to calculate.

Perhaps the highest cost of our careless extension of the use of imprisonment is the damage to thousands of people, most of whom have no prior prison record and who are convicted of petty crimes, and the future consequences of this damage to the society. These persons are being packed into dangerous, crowded prisons with minimal access to job training, education, or other services that will prepare them for life after prison. Some marginally involved petty criminals are converted into hard-core "outlaws"—mean, violence-prone convicts who dominate crowded prison wards.

Making matters worse, a growing number of prisoners are being subjected to extremely long sentences. These long-termers are not only stacking up in prisons and filling all available space, but their long terms, much of which they serve in maximum-security prisons that impose severe deprivation on them, result in more loss of social and vocational skills, more estrangement, and more alienation.

It must be kept in mind that virtually all of these profoundly damaged individuals will be released from prison and will try to pick up life on the outside. For the most part, their chances of pursuing a merely viable, much less satisfying, conventional life after prison are small. The contemporary prison experience has converted them into social misfits and cripples, and there is a growing likelihood that they will return to crime, violence, and other forms of disapproved deviance.

This ultimate cost of imprisonment—that which society must suffer when prisoners are released—continues to be confirmed by research. The Rand Corporation study cited earlier found that convicted felons sent to prison or granted probation had significantly higher rates of rearrest after release than those on probation.[27] In California, which has by far the nation's most overcrowded prison system, the recidivism rate (the rate of reimprisonment of prisoners released on parole), has doubled in the last five years.

Even more tragically, imprisonment is increasingly falling on blacks, Hispanics, and other people of color. Sixty years ago, almost one-fourth of all prison admissions were nonwhite. Today, nearly half of all prison admissions are nonwhite. Nationally, the imprisonment rate of blacks is at least ten times higher than for whites. Hispanics are incarcerated at a rate three times higher than whites. Studies show that a black male American has a 50 percent chance of being arrested once by age 29.[28]

OUR VINDICTIVE SOCIETY

Crime has incurred another profound cost: the increase of general vindictiveness in our society. Historically, Americans (as compared to Europeans and Japanese, for example) have been highly individualistic, which means, for one thing, that they are prone to blaming individuals for their actions. In America, according to the dominant ideology, everyone is responsible for his or her acts and every act is accomplished by a willful actor. Consequently, every undesirable, harmful, "bad" act is the work of a blameful actor. This belief has resulted in our being the most litigious people in the world and has given us the world's largest legal profession. It has also led us to criminalize more and more behavior and to demand more and more legal action against those who break laws. Today many Americans want someone blamed and punished for every transgression and inconvenience they experience.

Social science should have taught us that all human behavior is only partially a matter of free will and that persons are only partially responsible for their deeds. Everyone's actions are always somewhat influenced or dominated by factors not of one's own making and beyond personal control (with economic situation being the most influential and obvious).

Moreover, seeking vengeance is a pursuit that brings more frustration than satisfaction. It has not only been an obstacle in solving many social problems and in developing cooperative, communal attitudes (the lack of which are one of the important causes of the crime problem), but it is in itself a producer of excessive amounts of anxiety and frustration. Ultimately, vindictiveness erects barriers between people, isolates them, and prevents them from constructing the cooperative, communal social organizations that are so necessary for meaningful, satisfying human existence. Ironically, it is just these social structures that contain the true solution to our crime problem.

THE CRIME PROBLEM AS A DIVERSION

Our tendency toward vindictiveness is greatly nurtured by the media, politicians, and other public figures who have persistently harangued on the crime issue. They do this largely because the crime issue is seductive. It is seductive to politicians because they can divert attention away from larger and more pressing problems, such as the economy and pollution, whose solution would require unpopular sacrifices, particularly for them and other more affluent segments of the society.[29] Street crime is seductive to the media because it fits their preferred "sound bite" format of small bits of sensational material. Likewise, it is deeply seductive to the public, who, though they fear crime, possess at the same time deep fascination for it.

IT'S ABOUT TIME

We *must* turn away from the excessive use of prisons. The current incarceration binge will eventually consume large amounts of tax money, which will be diverted from essential public services such as education, child care, mental health, and medical services—the very same services that will have a far greater impact on reducing crime than building more prisons. We will continue to imprison millions of people under intolerably cruel and dangerous conditions. We will accumulate a growing number of ex-convicts who are more or less psychologically and socially crippled and excluded from conventional society, posing a continuing nuisance and threat to others. We will severely damage some of our more cherished humanitarian values, which are corroded by our excessive focus on blame and vengeance. And we will further divide our society into the white affluent classes and a poor nonwhite underclass, many of them convicts and ex-convicts. In effect, we are gradually putting our own apartheid into place.

We believe that these trends can be reversed without jeopardizing public safety. But how should we accomplish a turnaround of this magnitude? First, we must recognize that crime can, at best, be marginally reduced by escalating the use of imprisonment. If we are to truly reduce crime rates, we as a society must embark on a decade-long strategy that reverses the social and economic trends of the previous decade. In particular, we must jettison the overly expensive and ineffective criminal justice approach and redirect our energies on the next generation of youth, who already are at risk for becoming the generation of criminals.

The "crime reduction" reforms we have in mind have little to do with criminal justice reform. Rather, these reforms would serve to reduce poverty, single-parent families headed by females, teenage pregnancies and abortions, welfare dependency, unemployment, high dropout rates, drug abuse, and inadequate health care. These, and not "slack" imprisonment policies, are the social indicators that have proven to be predictive of high crime rates.[30]

The programs and policies that will work, such as better prenatal health care for pregnant mothers, better health care for children to protect them against life-threatening illnesses, Head Start, Job Corps, and Enterprise Zones, have been well documented.[31] We will also need a level of commitment from our major corporate leaders to reduce the flight of jobs, especially the so-called blue-collar and industrial jobs, from this country to Third World nations where cheap labor can be exploited for profits but at tremendous cost to this country. Given the current fiscal crisis facing most states and the federal government, however, it will be extremely difficult to continue a traditional and increasingly expensive war against crime and at the same time launch new social and economic policies that will reduce crime rates in the long term.

So how do we go about cutting our losses? We begin by reducing, or at least reducing the rate of growth in, the prison population and reallocating those "savings" to prevention programs targeted at at-risk youth and their families. But is it realistic to assume that prison populations and their associated costs can be lowered without increasing crime? How, exactly, should we proceed?

Many methods of reducing prison populations have been advocated. Some argue that certain classes of felony crimes should be reclassified as misdemeanors or decriminalized completely. In the late 1960s, there was a great deal of support to do this for many minor drug offenses. Others claim that a significant number of those convicted of felonies could be diverted from prison to probation and new forms of alternatives to prison, including intensive probation, house arrest, electronic surveillance, and greater use of fines and restitution.

We are persuaded, however, that these "front-end" reforms would not substantially reduce prison crowding. Historically, well-intentioned alternatives have had marginal impact on reducing prison populations. Instead, they have had the unintended consequence of widening the net of criminal justice by imposing more severe sanctions on people who otherwise would not be sentenced to prison.[32] Moreover, they have little support with public officials, who, like the public, are increasingly disenchanted with probation and other forms of community sanctions.

For alternatives to work, legislators, prosecutors, police, judges, and correctional agencies would all have to agree on new laws and policies to implement them. Such a consensus is unlikely to occur in the near future, since these measures are replete with controversy and disagreement. Even if the forces that are presently driving the punitive response to crime abated considerably, it would take several years to work through these disagreements and effect changes in the laws and policies that would slowly produce an easing of prison population growth. Such a slow pace of reform would not allow states to avoid the catastrophe that is rapidly developing in our prisons.

Even diversion of a substantial number of offenders from prison would not have a major impact on prison population growth. "Front-end" diversion reforms are targeted for those few offenders who are already serving the shortest prison terms (usually less than a year). The recent flood of tougher sentencing laws has greatly lengthened prison terms for offenders charged with more serious crimes and repeat property or drug offenders. Consequently, it is this segment of the prison population that is piling up in the prisons. The problem is that inmates with long sentences are unlikely to be candidates for diversion from prison.[33]

For these reasons, we believe the single most direct solution that would have an immediate and dramatic impact on prison crowding and would not affect public safety is to *shorten prison terms.* This can be done swiftly and fairly through a number of existing mechanisms, such as greater use of existing good-time credit statutes and/or accelerating parole eligibility.

Indeed, many states have launched such programs with no impact on crime rates. Between 1980 and 1983, the Illinois Director of Corrections released more than 21,000 prisoners an average of 90 days early because of severe prison crowding. The impact on the state's crime rate was insignificant, yet the program saved almost $50 million in tax dollars. A study of the program found that the amount of crime that could be attributed to early release was less than 1 percent of the total crime of the state. In fact, the state's crime rate actually *declined* while the early release program was in effect. Based on these findings, the state expanded its use of "good time" by another 90 days. A recent study of that expanded program found that the state was now saving over $90 million per year in state funds, even taking into account the costs of early release crimes (which represented less than one percent of all crimes committed in Illinois) to crime victims.[34] The governor has declared that no more new prisons will be built in Illinois.

An earlier demonstration of how swiftly and easily prison populations can be reduced occurred in California from 1967 to 1970. When Ronald Reagan became governor, he instructed the parole board to reduce the prison population. The board began shortening sentences, which it had the power to do within the indeterminate sentence system, and in two years lowered the prison population from 28,000 to less than 18,000.

Many other states are following these examples.[35] A recent study of the Oklahoma preparole program found that inmates could be released earlier by three to six months without influencing the state's crime rate and at considerable savings to the state. Specifically, that study found that for each inmate released early, the state saved over $9,000 per inmate, even when taking into account the costs of crimes committed by these offenders had they remained in prison.[36] Texas, Tennessee, and Florida are just a few states that have been required by the federal courts to reduce overcrowded prison systems by shortening prison terms.

For such a policy to work, prison terms would have to be shortened across the board, including inmates serving lengthy sentences for crimes of violence who, because of their age, no longer pose a threat to public safety. Since the average prison stay in the United States is approximately two years, even marginal reductions in the length of stay for large categories of inmates would have substantial effects on population size. Using the 1990 figure of approximately 325,000 new prison sentences, and assuming that 80 percent of those inmates (representing those who are nonviolent and have satisfactory prison conduct records) had their prison terms reduced by 30 days, the nation's prison population would have declined by 27,000 inmates. A 90-day reduction would result in 80,000 fewer prisoners; a six-month reduction, 160,000 fewer prisoners. Assuming an conservative average cost of $25,000 per inmate, the nation would avert as much as $4 billion a year in operating costs and reduce the need to construct new prisons.

Unless such a reform is adopted, prison populations as well as crime rates will continue to rise indefinitely into the twenty-first century. Reducing prison terms by the amounts advocated may only slow the rate of expansion. But it can be done with no cost to public safety and with enormous dollar savings. Most important, these averted costs can be redirected to more promising social reforms targeted at high-risk and disadvantaged youth and their families. Only by cutting our losses on our failed policy of unchecked punishment and imprisonment can we adequately address those social and economic forces that feed America's crime problem.

NOTES

1. As mentioned earlier, a consensus that rehabilitation did not work was reached in the early 1970s. Since then, many persons have reexamined the reports on treatment attempts, particularly those that were planned and implemented after the early 1960s and have argued many programs do work. Even Robert Martinson, the author of the article "What Works?" (*Public Interest* 35 [1974]: 22–54) and a coauthor with Lipton and Wilks of *The Effectiveness of Correctional Treatment: A Survey of Treatment Evaluation Studies* (New York: Preager, 1975), which were the culminating criticisms of treatment effectiveness, retracted his hard position in a latter review of the literature: "New Findings, New Views: A Note of Caution Regarding Sentencing Reform" (*Hofstra Law Review* 7 [1979]: 243–258). See also Francis T. Cullen and Paul Gendreau, "The Effectiveness of Correctional Rehabilitation: Reconsidering the 'Nothing Works' Debate," (in Lynn Goodstein and Doris McKenzie, eds., *The American Prison: Issues in Research and Policy* [New York: Plenum Press, 1989]). In general, what Martinson, Cullen, Gendreau and others have found in reexamining the treatment literature is that programs that emphasize learning and "cognitive" rather than medical or emotional disturbance models appear to reduce recidivism significantly.
2. See D. McDonald, *The Price of Punishment* (Boulder, Colo.: Westview Press, 1980) and Carl Loeb, "The Cost of Jailing in New York City," *Crime and Delinquency* (October 1978): 446–452.
3. See Bruce Cory and Stephen Gettinger, *Time to Build? The Realities of Prison Construction* (New York: Edna McConnell Clark Foundation, 1984).
4. See Loeb, "Cost of Jailing," 1978.

5. Identifying the true operating costs of a prison can be a very difficult task. The Criminal Justice Institute 1986 survey reported ranges of $7,023 to $30,909 from the various states, with an average cost of $14,591. However, this "average" underestimates the true average cost due to overcrowding that now plagues a majority of the state prison systems. As prisons become more crowded, the average cost per prisoner is temporarily lowered as the prisons handle more prisoners without greatly expanding their staff and other significant cost producers. But when construction and expansion of the system catch up (if they do), the cost per prisoner will be higher.
6. See Cory and Gettinger, *Time to Build?,* 1984.
7. See Steven D. Dillingham, Director, Bureau of Justice Statistics, "Remarks: The Attorney General's Summit on Law Enforcement Responses to Violent Crime: Public Safety in the Nineties," March 4–5, 1991, Washington, D.C.
8. Crime in the United States is measured by two different methods. The first is the Uniform Crime Reports (UCR), which includes all crimes reported to the police and tabulated by the FBI. The UCR only captures a limited number of crimes (homicide, rape, aggravated assault, robbery, burglary, larceny theft, and motor vehicle theft). A second method involves annual surveys conducted by the Census Bureau of persons living in households to determine how many households have been victimized by one of seven crimes (rape, robbery, assault, personal theft, household theft, burglary, and motor vehicle theft) each year. This crime reporting system, known as the National Crime Victim Survey or the NCVS, began in 1973. It should be noted that the NCVS does not include crimes against businesses (shoplifting, commercial burglaries), drug crimes, homicides, or crimes against children under the age of 12. Furthermore, the NCVS tends to record a large number of trivial crimes that are ordinarily not reported to the police.

   The UCR, unlike the NCVS, does include homicides, crimes committed against businesses or commercial properties, and crimes committed against children under the age of 12 and those not living in households. For these reasons, most criminologists believe that the UCR is a more reliable measure of crime.

For a review of the methodological merits of the UCR and NVCS, see Darrell Steffensmeier and Miles Harer, "Did Crime Rise or Fall During the Reagan Presidency?" *Journal of Research in Crime and Delinquency* 28, 3 (1991): 330–359.

9. See Dillingham, "Remarks."
10. See Steffensmeier and Harer, "Did Crime Rise or Fall?"
11. U.S. Department of Justice, *Crime and the Nation's Households, 1991* (Washington, D.C.: Office of Justice Programs, Bureau of Justice Statistics, July 1992), pp. 5–6.
12. We have been in close contact with a group of sociologists who have been studying drug use and trafficking in urban centers for the last ten years. This group includes Marsha Rosenbaum, Jeffery Fagan, Patrick Biernacki, Dan Waldorf, Paul Goldstein, and Shielga Murphy. They report to us there has been a dramatic shift from stealing to dealing drugs in the last decade.
13. *Dallas Morning Review,* February 12, 1992.
14. William Barr, *Combating Violent Crime: 24 Recommendations to Strengthen Criminal Justice,* Washington, D.C.: U.S. Department of Justice, Office of the Attorney General, July 22, 1992.
15. The UCR reports do not break down its national arrest data by felony and misdemeanor categories. However, California reports that approximately 30 percent of all adult arrests are felony level crimes (see *Crime and Delinquency in California, 1991,* Sacramento, CA: Office of the Attorney General, California Department of Justice, 1992, p. 121.) Furthermore, based on data reported in the Uniform Crime Reports, (*Crime in the United States, 1991,* p. 213 and p. 295), a total of 535,629 sworn police officers made a total of 14,211,900 arrests or an average of 26.5 arrests per officer.
16. California reports that approximately 65 percent of all adult felony arrests result in a conviction (see *Crime and Delinquency in California, 1991,* Sacramento, CA: Office of the Attorney General, California Department of Justice, 1992, p. 150).
17. California reports that approximately 19 percent of all adult felony arrests result in a prison sentence (see *Crime and Delinquency in California, 1991,* Sacramento, CA: Office of the Attorney General, California Department of Justice, 1992, p. 156).

18. Assuming $56,435 per medium-security cell constructed. This figure is based on 1991 costs as reported by Criminal Justice Institute, Inc., *The Correctional Yearbook,* Salem, NY: Criminal Justice Institute, Inc., 1992, p. 45. This figure also assumes that all prison construction is paid without the use of any revenue bonds.

19. Assuming an annual operating costs of imprisonment of $48.51 per day (Criminal Justice Institute, Inc., *The Correctional Yearbook,* Salem, NY: Criminal Justice Institute, Inc., 1992, p. 50.)

20. National Conference of State Legislatures, *State Budget Actions, 1992,* Washington, DC: National Conference of State Legislatures, Fiscal Affairs Program, December 1992, p. 29.

21. Bureau of Prisons, *1990 Census, Race and Hispanic Origin by Age and Sex for the United States, Regions, and States,* Washington, DC: Bureau of the Census, Racial Statistics Branch, 1992 and Bureau of Justice Statistics, *Sourcebook of Criminal Statistics, 1991,* Table 6.82.

22. Arnold S. Linsky and Murray Strauss, *Social Stress in the United States* (Dover, Mass.: Auburn House, 1986).

23. Robert J. Sampson and John H. Laub, *Crime in the Making: Pathways and Turning Points Through Life,* Cambridge, MA: Harvard University Press.

24. Claude Brown, "Manchild 1984," *This World,* September 23, 1984, pp. 7–8.

25. Jack Katz in a study of street criminals found that the excitement of criminal behavior was one of the strong attractions it holds for many offenders (*Seductions in Crime,* N.Y.: Basic Books, 1990).

26. "If Police Call It Gang Crime, That Doesn't Make It True," *Los Angeles Times,* September 28, 1989, part II, p. 7.

27. Joan Petersilia and Susan Turner, *Prison Versus Probation in California: Implications for Crime and Offender Recidivism* (Santa Monica, Calif.: Rand Corporation, 1986).

28. Robert Tillman, "The Prevalence and Incidence of Arrest Among Adult Males in California" (Sacramento: California State Attorney General, 1987); and James Austin and William Pannell, *The Growing Imprisonment of California* (San Francisco, Calif.: National Council on Crime and Delinquency, 1987).

29. When he was U.S. Attorney General under Ronald Reagan, Edwin Meese was one of the best examples of a powerful politician who made great use of the crime issue to divert attention. Throughout his public career, he barely avoided prosecution on various charges involving his and his friends receiving money illegally. All the while he persistently harangued about the crime problem, defined it as a problem of career criminals, and called for more punitive action, even suspension of constitutional procedures in order to keep career criminals in prison. In April 1988, the press reported on his possible involvement in the Wadtech scandal, which has led to the conviction of several persons, one a very close personal friend of Meese. In the midst of all this he delivered a speech to the nation's mayors in which he again fulminated against the new dangerous criminals, drug users.
30. For a comprehensive analysis of how these factors have been shown to be predictive of crime and mental illness in our society, see Linsky and Strauss, *Social Stress.*
31. See Lisbeth Schorr and Daniel Schorr, *Within Our Reach* (New York, NY: Anchor Books, 1990), for an exhaustive list of such programs and policies.
32. See James Austin and Barry Krisberg, "The Unmet Promise of Alternatives to Incarceration, *Crime and Delinquency* 28, 3 (1983): 374–409.
33. In Ohio, for example, which sentences almost half of its inmates to prison terms of less than one year, the state would reduce the prison population by only 10 percent if it diverted these inmates from prison to probation or jail.
34. James Austin and Melissa Bolyard, *The Effectiveness of Shorter Prison Terms* (San Francisco, Calif.: National Council on Crime and Delinquency, March 1993).
35. See James Austin, "The Use of Early Release and Sentencing Guidelines to Ease Prison Crowding," paper prepared for the National Academy of Sciences Conference on Prison and Jail Crowding. Chicago, Illinois, 1986.
36. See James Austin and Patricia Hardyman, *The Use of Early Parole with Electronic Monitoring to Control Prison Crowding* (San Francisco, Calif.: National Council on Crime and Delinquency, 1992).

Index

Numbers in italic refer to tables and figures.